THE LEARNING LANDSCAPE

HOW TO INCREASE LEARNER AGENCY AND BECOME A LIFELONG LEARNER

JAMES ANDERSON

First published in 2019 by Hawker Brownlow

This edition published in 2023 by James Anderson

© James Anderson 2023
The moral rights of the author have been asserted

The term "Challenge Pit" is a registered trade mark of Creative by Design Australia, Pty Ltd.

All rights reserved. Except as permitted under the Australian Copyright Act 1968 (for example, a fair dealing for the purposes of study, research, criticism or review), no part of this book may be reproduced, stored in a retrieval system, communicated or transmitted in any form or by any means without prior written permission.

All inquiries should be made to the author.

ISBN: 978-0-6459129-2-0

Illustrations © 2023 James Anderson.
Cover image © 2023 James Anderson.

Disclaimer
The material in this publication is of the nature of general comment only, and does not represent professional advice. It is not intended to provide specific guidance for particular circumstances and it should not be relied on as the basis for any decision to take action or not take action on any matter which it covers. Readers should obtain professional advice where appropriate, before making any such decision. To the maximum extent permitted by law, the author and publisher disclaim all responsibility and liability to any person, arising directly or indirectly from any person taking or not taking action based on the information in this publication.

SUPPORT FOR THE LEARNING LANDSCAPE

I have been a keen supporter of James Anderson's work for several years, and I was not disappointed by his latest work. *The Learning Landscape* is a key practice-focused exploration and synthesis of the range of ideas commonly used by educators. As James writes, growth mindsets, Habits of Mind, acquisition of excellence and antifragile "are not simply four good ideas" but rather their "authors observed and recognised them as real aspects of the human condition". *The Learning Landscape* supports improved understanding and enriched practice for educators by placing all these potentially powerful ideas, metaphors and frameworks in appropriate relation to each other. This is essential reading for all educators who what to dig deeper into the concepts of growth, learning dispositions and the need to support students' development of the learning process.

—Alex Delaforce, Head of Teaching and Learning,
Coomera Anglican College, Queensland

The Learning Landscape is an effective metaphor that makes the learning process visible and tangible. James Anderson uses metaphors and stories, along with his own refined personal reflections, to bring this book to life. He has mastered the art of making the research practical and easy to understand and implement. In particular, the Teacher Action sections make this book particularly relevant and useful for all educators.

—Luke McKenna, Former Assistant Principal,
Brisbane Catholic Education and Director of Unleashing Personal Potential

THE LEARNING LANDSCAPE

James Anderson deepens the conversation of growth in education by providing an accessible guide that explains the process of learning for everyone in your educational community, including teachers, leaders, students and parents. It supports how we can help students, and even ourselves as teachers, know themselves as lead learners – empowering them to decide what steps they need to take next. *The Learning Landscape* is brilliant in its simplicity and nuanced depth at the same time!

—Lee Kynaston, Head of Student Development,
Pimlico State High School, Queensland

The Learning Landscape moves with agility through the mountains and valleys of learning, following an itinerary set by the theories of Dweck's growth mindset, Costa's and Kallick's Habits of Mind, Ericsson's peak performance and Taleb's antifragility. What is remarkable is how the synthesis of these theories seeds rich and fertile ideas for framing teaching and learning that supports the fundamental concept that students don't grow without being nurtured. The ideas James presents are stimulating and their translation to practice is useful immediately – at its heart, *The Learning Landscape* is a call to action!

—Arthur L. Costa, Professor Emeritus, California State University, Sacramento,
and Bena Kallick, Co-Founder and Co-Director of Institute for Habits of Mind,
Program Director for Eduplanet21.com

CONTENTS

Introduction vii
    What's in it for Learners?.. viii
    What's in it for Teachers? ix

Chapter 1: The Learning Landscape 1
    Features of the Learning Landscape 2
    A Map of the Learning Landscape 3
    Learning in the Learning Landscape 7
    The Learners 9
    Teacher Action: Explaining the Learning Landscape 12
    Nadia Comăneci: Great, Not Good 13

Chapter 2: Learners 17
    Above-the-Line and Below-the-Line Learners......................... 20
    Defining Success 25
    Experience versus Expertise 26
    Backstories 27
    Six Types of Learners 28
    Teacher Action: Developing Learners 33
    Picasso: The Value of Backstory 34
    Mozart: The Hidden Backstory 36

Chapter 3: Challenge 41
    Near Side and Far Side 42
    Types of Challenges.. 43
    The Real Benefit of Climbing 51
    How Different Learners Relate to Their Learning Zone 51
    Antifragile 54
    Teacher Action: Setting the Challenge 55
    About Learning Challenges and Learning Pits™ 56

THE LEARNING LANDSCAPE

Chapter 4: Habits of Mind 61
    What Goes in a Backpack? 62
    Becoming a Better Climber 64
    Developing the Habits of Mind 66
    The Benefits of Becoming a Better Climber 69
    How Different Learners Relate to Their Backpack 70
    Opportunities 73
    Teacher Action: Filling the Backpack 75
    Turia Pitt 76

Chapter 5: Practice 79
    Virtuous Practice 80
    Climbing 81
    How Different Learners Relate to Mistakes and Feedback 88
    Teacher Action: Guiding the Climb 91

Chapter 6: Mindset 93
    About Mindsets 94
    Symptoms of Mindset 94
    The Mindset Continuum 97
    Growth Mindset and Growth 99
    Changing Mindsets 103
    Teacher Action: Mindset Movers 109
    Why Many Growth Mindset Interventions Fail 114

Chapter 7: Effort 117
    About Effort 118
    Effective Effort Matrix 119
    How Different Learners Respond to Effort 121
    Teacher Action: Effort 126

Conclusion 129
Glossary 133
List of Figures 139
Endnotes 141
About the Author 143

INTRODUCTION

WELCOME TO THE LEARNING LANDSCAPE!

The Learning Landscape is a powerful metaphor for learning. It draws a parallel between the abstract cognitive world of learning and the physical journey of exploring the real world. By doing this, it makes the learning process more tangible, more concrete and, therefore, more accessible to learners.

But this metaphor is not simply a nice story intended to entertain. It is a tool, a logical argument, to help both learners and educators understand learning and the learning process. And in this capacity, it excels.

The Learning Landscape allows us to visualise learning as a journey through the rich landscape of knowledge and understandings. As we venture far and wide in the Learning Landscape, we explore all areas of human knowledge. Climbing towards the highest peaks develops expertise.

Throughout the journey, learners encounter challenges in the form of "pits". We learn that not all challenges are the same. Downhill and Performance Challenges do not gain the learner any height in the Learning Landscape. Only the Learning Challenge provides a path towards expertise.

Importantly, in order to explore the Learning Landscape and succeed when attempting Learning Challenges, learners must become effective climbers, developing new skills to allow them to explore more complex understandings.

The metaphor is used to illustrate four significant areas of research, each critical to developing successful learners. These are:
- Antifragile (Nassim Nicholas Taleb)
- Habits of Mind (Art Costa and Bena Kallick)
- Acquisition of Excellence (Anders Ericsson)
- Mindset (Carol Dweck).

THE LEARNING LANDSCAPE

These are not simply four good ideas. They were not dreamed up by the authors. The authors observed and recognised them as real aspects of the human condition.

This is why the Learning Landscape metaphor is so powerful. Unlike the latest literacy strategy or the exciting new program to teach science (both of which might be practical and useful), these ideas are real. They are embedded in our human condition, observed and described by these authors. Collectively, they describe what it means to develop Learner Agency and become an increasingly efficacious learner.

WHAT'S IN IT FOR LEARNERS?

By embedding the above ideas into the metaphor of the Learning Landscape, we make them tangible and accessible for learners. Learning is seen as moving through the Learning Landscape. Expertise is realised by climbing the highest peaks. Along the way, learners encounter challenges of different shapes and sizes in the form of Challenge Pits. The struggle of learning and the skilfulness required are represented by the climb out of the Challenge Pit, facilitated by the tools and strategies learners carry in their backpack. Finally, learners recognise how to become more skilful learners by becoming better "climbers".

By providing students with this broad metaphor for their learning, it helps them understand that the point of all this learning is not simply to know more but to become better learners. By becoming better learners, they ultimately have more choice in life. They have the capacity to pursue their own goals and face adversity – to roam freely through the Learning Landscape.

WHAT'S IN IT FOR TEACHERS?

Educators will find the Learning Landscape gives them a concrete and practical way of talking about the learning process with learners. It provides you with a metacognitive language all students can relate to, making them more aware of the learning process and helping you achieve greater learning outcomes. You'll find your classrooms come alight with conversations about learning rather than simply focusing on what's being learned.

You may find there are aspects of the Learning Landscape that challenge some of your assumptions about learning. If this happens, I encourage you to go further and read more of the work by Taleb, Costa and Kallick, Ericsson and Dweck and understand the learning process more deeply.

INTRODUCTION

Many educators have been raised with very fixed ideas about intelligence. These educators will see some students face barriers in the Learning Landscape, stopping their exploration of parts of the Learning Landscape (see *Chapter 6: Mindset*).

The metaphor of the Learning Landscape challenges those fixed ideas and puts the onus on what the learner does, not on who they are, for successful learning. It describes how all learners are capable of traversing the Learning Landscape far and wide to become an expert. With this in mind, some educators will be challenged to expect even more of their learners and to do more to prepare them better to reach and exceed these expectations.

Perhaps most importantly for educators, the Learning Landscape helps us understand why some learners are more efficacious than others. By shining a light on the types of behaviours that lead to more effective learning, educators are better able to describe individual learners and provide formative feedback to guide students to become better learners.

Lastly, remember that the Learning Landscape is a metaphor. Like all metaphors, it is useful until it isn't. It provides a powerful and practical way of talking about the broad learning process and how to become a better learner. But if you push the metaphor too far, it will break. That said, I think you'll find you can push it a long way before that happens.

We will begin by looking at the broad features of the Learning Landscape as we explore how knowledge and complexity are represented in the Learning Landscape. We'll then look at how learners move through and explore this landscape, paying particular attention to why some learners are better equipped to climb the highest peaks than others.

The Learning Landscape presents learners with challenges in the form of four different types of Challenge Pits. We explore the importance of "filling your backpack" to equip learners to succeed at these challenges and ultimately climb out the pit. We then explore the impact of mindset on our journey through the Learning Landscape to explain why some learners perceive boundaries and limits to their learning. Finally, we give a new definition to effort and explain why not all effort is equal.

LET'S BEGIN.

CHAPTER 1
THE LEARNING LANDSCAPE

The Learning Landscape is a metaphor to help learners and teachers think about *where* learning takes place.

This chapter is about gaining an initial understanding of the broad features of the Learning Landscape that we'll be travelling through and exploring throughout the rest of this book. Consider this chapter a broad overview of the Learning Landscape and the learners to be found within. We are going to get the "lay of the land", so to speak

We'll then begin to look at Learner Agency: how learners move through the Learning Landscape, exploring, discovering, climbing and, ultimately, learning more.

As we progress through this book and delve deeper into the Learning Landscape, we'll become more familiar with all of its aspects.

THE LEARNING LANDSCAPE

FEATURES OF THE LEARNING LANDSCAPE

Imagine the Learning Landscape as encompassing everything there is to know and understand about the world. Every fact, every understanding – all knowledge has a place in the Learning Landscape.

The Learning Landscape is not a crystal ball. It won't tell learners the future. It won't generate new ideas. There are no inventions in the Learning Landscape. Applying, analysing, evaluating, synthesising and creating – these are all things learners do with knowledge and understandings and are not found in the Learning Landscape.

But learners can find the knowledge and understandings to become better thinkers in the Learning Landscape. For example, they can learn how to evaluate, or how to get better at generating ideas. The Learning Landscape teaches learners *how* to think, but not *what* to think.

By travelling the length and breadth of the Learning Landscape, learners may explore the full extent and diversity of all knowledge and understandings. Moving north, south, east and west, to every point of the compass, learners uncover new understandings of not just what is already known, but also of everything that can be known. All knowledge and understandings exist here, waiting for learners to discover them.

Each generation pushes the boundaries of the Learning Landscape, slowly uncovering new territory, making discoveries and learning more about the world in which we live. As we'll discuss later, these explorers are often Agile Learners – well-equipped to reach new heights and explore new land within the Learning Landscape.

Each learner must explore the Learning Landscape for themselves. While this is made easier by those who have gone before us and can show us the way, it is up to the individual to travel the Learning Landscape for themselves and acquire the knowledge and understandings they need to lead the life they want to lead.

For example, although we know the workings of a rocket engine are understood and form part of our collective Learning Landscape, an individual learner may not have explored that part of the Learning Landscape personally. There is a difference between the collective Learning Landscape and what a learner has explored for themselves.

Our school curriculum represents what we have decided is most important for learners to explore and master at school. It is a tiny portion of the entire Learning Landscape. As lifelong learners, we could spend our lives exploring the Learning Landscape – ranging far and wide, climbing mountains, learning new things – and only ever cover a fraction of everything there is to learn. The Learning Landscape is vast!

CHAPTER 1: THE LEARNING LADDER

A MAP OF THE LEARNING LANDSCAPE

It would be tempting – and, at times, useful – to divide the Learning Landscape into areas, in the same way we divide the world into countries. These countries would represent different areas of knowledge: maths, science, language, history, art, etc. Closely related areas would lie next to each other.

For example, learning to add single-digit numbers would be in the same general area as all other maths, not far from algebra and calculus. Forming simple sentences would be in a different part of the Learning Landscape, a long way from maths, and closer to poetry.

But as in the real world, while we might find it useful to think of different areas of knowledge as has having defined boundaries, these boundaries don't exist. All areas of knowledge and understanding are connected in one way or another and learners can move freely across all areas of the Learning Landscape.

Learners don't need a passport or visa to move around the Learning Landscape. This is important to remember, as in the past it has been common for learners to specialise in one small area of the Learning Landscape. A learner would become an expert in economics or a master of art. But increasingly, the problems we need today's learners to address draw on multiple disciplines, so learners must be able to cover many different parts of the Learning Landscape. The most successful learners in the 21st century will be the ones who can roam far and wide in the Learning Landscape and don't restrict themselves to one area.

HILLS AND MOUNTAINS, PLAINS AND PLATEAUS

Like the real landscape, the Learning Landscape is not flat and featureless. It contains hills and mountains, plains and plateaus. There are soaring peaks that disappear into the clouds, their heights unknowable. Because of these features, exploring the Learning Landscape can be challenging. Some knowledge and understandings take great skill and effort to acquire, while others are attained more easily.

In the Learning Landscape, difficulty is represented by height. The higher you go, the more complex and demanding are the knowledge and understandings that you encounter. For example, adding single-digit numbers or forming simple sentences are relatively simple tasks, so both are found closer to "sea level". Writing powerful speeches or doing advanced algebra are more complex tasks, so are located higher up the hills and mountains.

THE LEARNING LANDSCAPE

❶ CONTOUR LINES

On maps of the physical world, cartographers use contour lines to represent elevation. Sea level is used to represent zero, and each contour line represents the number of metres above sea level.

In the Learning Landscape, educators use contour lines to represent levels of difficulty – often referred to as "standards". The lowest contour line represents the most basic knowledge and understandings in an area. Each subsequent contour line represents an increase in the level of difficulty or complexity.

❷ HEIGHT REPRESENTS DIFFICULTY IN THE LEARNING LANDSCAPE

For example, a learner who is learning to count operates at some of the lowest contour lines. Learning to read their first 50 sight words is at a similar height but in a different part of the Learning Landscape. The more difficult tasks of addition and forming short sentences are found higher up, represented by higher contour lines.

In this way, you can think of year levels as represented by the major contour lines. The curriculum is arranged in such a way that each year is not about simply learning more, but it is also about mastering more difficult and complex understandings.

As we'll see in *Chapter 2: Learners*, some contour lines take on special significance for individual learners. They seem to limit their growth, but these limits are imagined. Learners can always climb higher in the Learning Landscape.

While the most basic understandings form the lowest areas of the Learning Landscape, they are far from being unimportant. They are foundational. All other knowledge and understandings are built upon them. Learners can't climb the highest peaks without starting in the lowlands! And, as we shall see in *Chapter 3: Challenges*, this foundational knowledge and all the knowledge learners acquire from the "land beneath our feet" is of critical importance to defining the sorts of challenges learners take on.

ABOUT "DIFFICULT"

It's important to note that when we talk about height representing difficulty and complexity in the Learning Landscape, this is only in relation to the difficulty and complexity of other knowledge and understandings, not the amount of challenge or effort involved in attaining this knowledge.

CHAPTER 1: THE LEARNING LADDER

Each step "up" from one contour line to the next requires a particular kind of effort (see *Chapter 7: Effort*). It doesn't matter where that step takes place; each new step upwards in the Learning Landscape presents what we describe in *Chapter 3: Challenges* as a Learning Challenge that requires effort and may involve struggle.

For example, moving from counting in single digits (1, 2, 3, 4 …) to adding (3 + 4 = 7) can pose as much of a challenge, and require as much effort from the learner, as moving from the higher contour lines of multiplying (6 × 2 = 12) to factorising (numbers that go into 12: 1, 2, 3, 4, 6).

While we often describe learning something new as being "difficult", what we really mean is that it presents a challenge requiring effort and struggle to overcome. As we'll explore throughout this book, climbing higher in the Learning Landscape to learn something more complex and difficult will always require a particular kind of effort. But learning something less difficult, something you can think of as going downhill, requires little true effort.

As we'll discuss in *Chapter 3: Challenges*, learning that results in increasing standards will always be challenging.

MAPS, ROADS, PATHS AND SIGNPOSTS

As well as the "natural" features of the Learning Landscape, there are also human-made features created by people who have previously explored that part of the Learning Landscape. Sometimes, these might take the form of detailed guidebooks, with clear paths outlining every step to ensure the quickest possible exploration of the Learning Landscape. At other times, there are only signposts pointing out a general direction in which the learner should head.

Our curriculum documents, everything from our F–12 guides to lesson plans, are maps. These documents represent broad roads through the Learning Landscape; routes that cover what our school systems consider the most important parts of the Learning Landscape.

In some parts of the Learning Landscape, the pathway to mastery is extremely well defined. Many people have already travelled it. Each step has been identified and the quickest, most effective route has been marked out.

THE LEARNING LANDSCAPE

An example of an extremely clear route to mastery is the Suzuki method of music practice. Each student is taken down the same path, learning in the same sequence. The Suzuki method has been proven to work time and time again. Similar pathways exist for other mature fields, such as karate, classical music, ballet and the Khan Academy for mathematics. Anders Ericsson uses the term "Deliberate Practice" to describe the journey of a learner who follows a well-worn path to a destination that others recognise as expertise.[1]

Other parts of the Learning Landscape are less well signposted. These are areas where there may be general principals to follow, but no single path to uniform, expert performance. Parenting and creative writing are examples of this type of learning. In these situations, you have to make your own way, creating your own path through the Learning Landscape. Ericsson calls this type of practice "Purposeful Practice".[2]

We'll explore both Deliberate and Purposeful Practice in *Chapter 5: Practice*.

NO FENCES. NO BOUNDARIES. NO LIMITS.

While it is important to recognise the features of the Learning Landscape, it is at least equally as important to recognise what features are absent.

There are no fences or boundaries in the Learning Landscape. Other than a limited life span, there's nothing to stop any learner from exploring all of the Learning Landscape. Learners are free to roam far and wide, high and low. There are no ceilings, no limits to potential, no point at which a learner can't continue learning to do harder things. It is always possible to explore and be a lifelong learner – although not many learners truly remain lifelong learners.

Unfortunately, many learners act as if there are limits to what they can learn. They build boundaries, telling themselves they can't go to a particular part of the Learning Landscape. They convince themselves they are not the right "type" of person to go to one place or another, or they place limits on how high they can climb, believing they don't have what it takes to climb any higher. We will explore these self-limiting beliefs in *Chapter 6: Mindset*.

Understanding the nature of the Learning Landscape is just the beginning of our story. The heart of this book is about increasing Learner Agency. It's understanding how to create better learners. So, let's look at what learning looks like, then begin to explore the different types of learners in the Learning Landscape.

CHAPTER 1: THE LEARNING LADDER

LEARNING IN THE LEARNING LANDSCAPE

In the Learning Landscape, learners move from one place to another. The more ground they cover, the more knowledge and understandings they acquire. In this way, learning in the Learning Landscape is about movement.

Teachers are familiar with the language of moving through the Learning Landscape. We talk about "moving on" to a new topic. This is analogous to moving to a new part of the Learning Landscape. We also talk about covering the curriculum, which is about ensuring a specific area of the Learning Landscape is explored.

Similarly, teachers often talk about the "learning journey". This represents the path we guide learners along, the challenges they encounter along the way, and the new learnings that occur as a result of that journey.

Learner Agency is a measure of how well learners move through the Learning Landscape. Increasing Learner Agency makes a person a better learner. Some learners equip themselves exceptionally well and can move freely through the Learning Landscape; they roam far and wide, climbing the highest mountains.

Unfortunately, some learners find it more difficult to move through the Learning Landscape or stop moving altogether. They become Non-Learners: static and stationary, never learning anything new. We will consider the different types of learners in *Chapter 2: Learners* and how we, as educators, can increase Learner Agency.

When learners move through the Learning Landscape, they can be said to be learning "more" things. This learning can occur by following well-worn paths and signposts or by exploring new territory. But it is not simply the "more" that we need to consider. The nature of what is being learned is of critical importance. We must ask: is what's being learned simply one more thing – something easily acquired – or is it something more difficult?

Whether a student is learning just one more thing or something more difficult is determined by whether the learner is moving uphill, downhill or sideways.

UP, DOWN OR SIDEWAYS?

Recall that in the Learning Landscape, contour lines represent the relative difficulty of what is being learned. Each step higher signifies something more complex and difficult.

THE LEARNING LANDSCAPE

Moving sideways means a student is learning something at the same level of difficulty as they had previously achieved. This occurs when they follow the same contour lines. They take a flat path or stay on the plains and plateaus of the Learning Landscape.

When a learner moves sideways, they are still learning something "new", but it is no more difficult than what they've mastered previously. Their *standard* stays the same. They are learning more, not learning something more difficult. Moving sideways does not require learners to become better learners.

There are many occasions in schools when we ask learners to move sideways. The result is "covering" a new topic. It demands little more from learners than the application of their current abilities to the new task. For example, in a geography unit, it might be important to cover the basic facts about several countries. The skills used to learn about one country are simply reapplied to learning the facts about another. It's not until the learner must apply these facts in more complex ways that they need to become better learners.

Moving downhill means learners are learning something less complex than what they've previously achieved. It might take some time, and they'll end up knowing something new, but the effort required to move downhill and master easier things does not stretch them. Like moving sideways, moving downhill only results in students learning more, not learning something more difficult.

Downhill learning can look like busy work. For example, the learner who has reached a certain standard but then chooses, or is given, problems of a lower standard is still working, but the learning does not challenge them, and they will almost inevitably find the task easy. They may cover a new part of the Learning Landscape, but they aren't stretching themselves.

Moving uphill is similar to moving sideways or downhill, in that the learner is learning something new. No matter which way they go, they will acquire new knowledge or understandings. The critical difference is that moving uphill means learning something more difficult than previously mastered. Going uphill raises the standard. As we will explore in *Chapter 2: Learners*, going uphill requires learners to increase Learner Agency and become better learners.

Uphill learning is the sort of learning we want learners to engage in much, but not all, of the time. We want them to master increasingly difficult tasks; to move from the foothills into the mountains. Ultimately, uphill learning can take learners to the highest peaks (or expertise).

CHAPTER 1: THE LEARNING LADDER

But to move uphill – to climb higher in the Learning Landscape and master something more difficult – learners must increase their Learner Agency and become better learners. It is not simply "moving" through the Learning Landscape that is important; learners must learn how to climb with great skill to achieve great heights. It's how learners engage in the Learning Process, how they climb, that is of critical importance.

It is also important to note that learning is not a simple matter. Learning is challenging. To move from one place to another in the Learning Landscape, learners must go through "pits". Depending on the nature of the challenge, these "Challenge Pits" may require learners to climb with great skill. We'll explore the concept of a Challenge Pit in *Chapter 3: Challenges* and throughout this book.

As educators, our job is not simply to lead learners through the Learning Landscape. We must also increase Learner Agency and teach learners how to become better learners. While it is important to understand the nature of the Learning Landscape and what it means to move through it, it is teaching learners *how* to move through the Learning Landscape most effectively that forms the core of this book. We must teach learners to become better climbers!

THE LEARNERS

The part of the Learning Landscape of most interest to educators is, of course, the learners. The Learning Landscape is populated with learners!

Chapter 2: Learners takes an in-depth look at the different types of learners we find in the Learning Landscape. In each chapter, we will look at how different learners behave in response to the Learning Landscape. Importantly, we'll look at the teacher actions required to help students increase Learner Agency and become better learners.

As we become familiar with the Learning Landscape, it's worth taking a step back to look at learners in a broader context. Who are they? Where do we find them? What are they doing? What are their similarities and differences?

WHERE DO WE FIND LEARNERS?

As we've already mentioned, the Learning Landscape encompasses everything we know, as well as everything that is knowable. So, while some areas are well-populated with learners, there are tracts of land with no learners at all. These areas represent future learning, as well as learnings that might have been lost.

THE LEARNING LANDSCAPE

As we take a bird's-eye view of the Learning Landscape, we notice there are more learners in the lowlands and fewer on the mountain peaks. Most learners can move freely throughout the lowlands of the Learning Landscape where the knowledge and understandings are simple and less complex. But at the higher altitudes, we find just a few individuals – the experts in their fields.

LIMITS AND BOUNDARIES

As noted earlier, there are no walls, fences or boundaries in the Learning Landscape. The strange thing is that some learners act as though there are.

Some learners stay in one domain of the Learning Landscape without venturing too far in any one direction. They limit themselves to one area of the map and seem unable to travel further. It's as if they've approached an invisible line in the Learning Landscape and can't go beyond it. These are the people who *categorise* themselves as "being" a particular type of person. They may believe they are artistic, mathematical or musical, and can therefore only move through that part of the Learning Landscape.

Other learners in the Learning Landscape limit themselves vertically. They get to a certain standard – a contour line – and are unwilling even to attempt to go above that line. These learners believe they aren't "smart enough" to try anything more difficult. As we'll discuss in *Chapter 4: Habits of Mind*, these learners are only half right. They currently may not be able to climb higher, but they are capable of learning how.

Other learners attempt to go above the line but appear unable to reach new heights. They have reached what we call a Learning Plateau. They get stuck at a certain height, not knowing how to proceed.

These boundaries, both horizontal and vertical, are imaginary. They exist only in the learner's imagination. As we'll discuss in *Chapter 6: Mindset*, self-limiting beliefs can have a significant impact on growth and achievement.

Of course, some learners choose to stay in one area of the Learning Landscape. They make it their home, spending their whole life finding out everything there is to know in that field. What makes these learners different from the ones discussed above is that they *choose* to stay in one part of the Learning Landscape. Other learners incorrectly believe they have no choice. There's a big difference between not travelling through part of the Learning Landscape because you don't want to, and not travelling through the Learning Landscape because you don't believe you can.

CHAPTER 1: THE LEARNING LADDER

CHILDREN AND ADULTS

The next thing we notice is there are learners of all ages. Learning does not stop when we leave school; it continues throughout life. But this is not to say all adults continue to learn.

It is interesting to note that children are found only in the lowlands, while adults are found high and low throughout the Learning Landscape. In short, there are no children in the mountains. Some children strike out for the hills and mountains, and a few seem a little further ahead than their peers, but none have reached any great heights. They are all still journeying through the lowlands.

At first glance, this might seem odd. But on closer inspection, it isn't odd at all. Climbing to the highest peaks, gaining all that knowledge and understanding takes time. In fact, it can take a lifetime to be considered an expert in your field. Children simply haven't had the time to do that yet. Nor have they had time to develop the skills required to negotiate the highest peaks.

There is a valuable insight to be gained here. Recall that in the Learning Landscape, difficulty, or standard, is represented by height and learning is represented by movement. As you climb higher, you reach greater and greater standards. In this way, standards, when applied to learners, represent *where* they are, not *who* they are.

Individual learners change their standard by climbing higher. The story of "Nadia Comăneci: Great, Not Good" at the end of this chapter helps us understand this point more clearly.

All children are born in the lowlands, which is why there are no children high up in the mountains. No-one is born with a map of the Learning Landscape installed in their head. Learners must create that map and make that journey themselves. To get to the mountains, learners must climb, and it takes time to develop the skills to do that. There are no short cuts. We'll learn more about this in *Chapter 2: Learners* and discuss the importance of the learner's "backstory" when we explore the stories of Mozart and Picasso.

THE LEARNING LANDSCAPE

TEACHER ACTION: EXPLAINING THE LEARNING LANDSCAPE

Discuss the Learning Landscape with students. Explain that all our knowledge and understandings are within the Learning Landscape. Emphasise that knowledge and understandings are in the Learning Landscape to be discovered – they are not in our heads to be unlocked.

Describe learning as a journey through the Learning Landscape. For each lesson, explain which part of the Learning Landscape learners will be exploring.

Help students recognise that the standard they are at represents where they are in the Learning Landscape and how high they have climbed, not who they are. Students who are at a higher standard have simply climbed higher. This might elicit conversations about being a better climber (see *Chapter 2: Learners* and *Chapter 4: Habits of Mind*).

Emphasise that there are no boundaries in the Learning Landscape. Ask students to discuss whether they think there are parts of the Learning Landscape they can't go to. Why? Discuss which parts of the Learning Landscape they are most familiar with. Why?

Help students recognise that their learning journey will be a long one. Today's learning is among the very first steps in a much longer journey.

Show students the learning path they will follow, emphasising that many others have already been down that path and explored that part of the Learning Landscape. Point out signposts along the way that point to different parts of the Learning Landscape to be explored another day.

Begin to distinguish between uphill and downhill learning. When have students engaged in uphill learning and when have they engaged in downhill learning? Introduce the idea that over time, you want all learners to become better climbers and climb higher in the Learning Landscape.

Recognise that in the Learning Landscape, all learners are essentially the same. The difference in learning outcomes is due to what each learner does, not who they are. Each learner is in charge of their journey through the Learning Landscape.

Use the story of Nadia Comăneci or other experts whose standards have been surpassed to highlight that standards are only where you are, not who you are. What Comăneci did was great because she was the first to do it – not because she was a unique person. We all follow the path of learners before us, making our journey easier. Comăneci's greatness was in leading the way. Now others can reach and exceed her standards.

CHAPTER 1: THE LEARNING LADDER

NADIA COMĂNECI: GREAT, NOT GOOD

Nadia Comăneci is a legend in the sport of gymnastics. In the 1976 Olympic Games in Montreal, she received seven perfect 10 scores – an unprecedented achievement.

Comăneci was a pioneer on the uneven bars. She was the first person to perform "release" moves, where she released the bar, performed a somersault and re-caught the same bar. Her routines included dismounts previously unseen and, at the time, were unmatched in their difficulty.

Her performances on the beam and floor were also groundbreaking and breathtaking because they contained elements never previously performed.

In short, Comăneci was like no other gymnast who had gone before. Her impact on the sport can't be underestimated. Her routines set the style and tone for female gymnastics for decades. And because the sport hadn't anticipated anyone could perform such difficult routines and to such a high level, it forced changes in how gymnastic routines were scored.

Comăneci was a great gymnast. But she wasn't a very good gymnast.

Take a moment to reflect on Comăneci's achievements. She was undoubtedly one of the greatest gymnasts of all time in terms of the impact she had on the sport. Equally, she was undoubtedly the very best gymnast of her time, performing at a standard and level of difficulty previously unseen.

But by today's standards, her routines would only be considered good. Today, a gymnast would be unlikely to make an Olympic team and certainly wouldn't win any gold medals with the routines Comăneci performed in 1976. Today's gymnasts are performing much more difficult routines and at a much higher standard.

In short, Comăneci had climbed higher in the Learning Landscape for gymnastics than anyone else at the time. This was what made her great. She stood higher than anyone else ever had. But since then, others have climbed higher.

THE LEARNING LANDSCAPE

This highlights the point that standards – your height in the Learning Landscape – are neither good nor bad. They only represent where you are, not who you are.

Although Comăneci was considered the best gymnast of her era, it was not because of who she was; rather, it was because she was the first to reach those standards. The standards didn't define her greatness, only being the first to arrive at them did. Today, other gymnasts of her standard are not considered great.

It is the nature of elite performance that we build upon what others have learned before us. Once someone has blazed a trail in the Learning Landscape, others can follow – and usually more quickly. This is equally true for academic and intellectual endeavours.

Comăneci no longer stands atop the highest mountain in gymnastics. Her standards have been surpassed. Many others now stand higher in terms of the standards they have achieved. The complexity and difficulty of today's routines far exceed what Comăneci achieved. She is no longer the best. But she is still one of the greatest.

The standard a learner is at does not define their greatness. Likewise, it does not lessen them. It is simply where they are. Today, gymnasts who repeated Comăneci's routines would be quietly congratulated for reaching that milestone, then told to continue the climb and get even better. In 1976, that standard made a gymnast the best in the world. Today, to be the best requires a gymnast do more.

Understanding that standards only represent where a learner is in the Learning Landscape, not who they are, can make them very humble. As we'll explore in *Chapter 6: Mindset*, when we discuss Roger Federer, it is one of the hallmarks of a Growth Mindset.

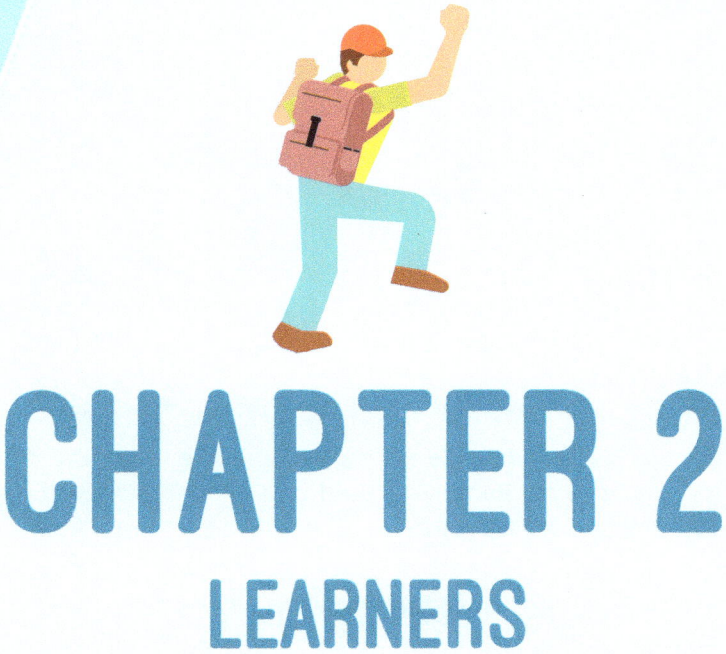

CHAPTER 2
LEARNERS

While all learners are essentially the same – no learner has a significant natural advantage over another – that does not mean all learners behave the same way or achieve the same things. Learners differ in how well they move through the Learning Landscape; a quality referred to as Learner Agency.

In this chapter, we introduce six different types of learners.

The Below-the-Line Learners, those who fail to stretch themselves and grow, are:
- Non-Learners
- Beginning Learners
- Performance Learners.

The Above-the-Line Learners, those who stretch and grow, improving their ability to move and climb higher in the Learning Landscape, are:
- Directed Learners
- Independent Learners
- Agile Learners.

THE LEARNING LANDSCAPE

WHAT ARE LEARNERS DOING?

Although there are learners throughout the Learning Landscape, closer inspection reveals they are not all *doing* the same things.

As mentioned earlier, some "learners" – if we can call them that – aren't moving at all. They are usually in the lowlands, not moving far and certainly not through any part of the Learning Landscape they haven't already explored. They aren't learning anything new. These are Non-Learners.

Fortunately, there are few true Non-Learners. Most people in the Learning Landscape are moving. They acquire new knowledge and understandings, even if they are not roaming far or climbing great heights.

But these learners vary greatly in how effectively they move. Some seem to confidently stride forward into new parts of the Learning Landscape, striking out for the highest peaks. Others struggle, progressing more slowly. Different learners behave in different ways and, as a result, some are more effective at moving through the Learning Landscape than others.

There are a few learners who can strike out for the highest peaks and change direction when needed. They respond to challenges and adversity more effectively than others, even leveraging challenges to help them grow. These are Agile Learners.

For now, the important point is that the key difference between learners is *what they do*, not who they are.

EQUIPMENT

As we take a closer look at learners, we notice something else. They all carry backpacks. To be more accurate, some carry satchels, some carry day packs and others carry backpacks. For the sake of consistency, we'll refer to all these as "backpacks". These backpacks are full of equipment that help the learner move through the Learning Landscape. In short, some learners are better equipped than others.

We will discuss in detail what's in these backpacks and how learners can fill them in *Chapter 4: Habits of Mind*. For now, what's important to note is that only those with the biggest backpacks, those who are the best equipped, reach the highest standards and peaks. No-one stands on top of a mountain of expertise with a day pack.

CHAPTER 2: LEARNERS

Learners carrying satchels and small day packs seem to be restricted to exploring only the lowlands of the Learning Landscape. They are poorly equipped so are unable to venture into the more complex and difficult areas higher up in the mountains.

It's interesting to note that those with the biggest backpacks are not restricted to the highest peaks. Many well-equipped learners roam the foothills and lower peaks. They confidently move through these areas on their learning journeys. Some have climbed high in one area of the Learning Landscape and are now setting off to conquer mountains somewhere new. (See the story about Turia Pitt in *Chapter 4: Habits of Mind* for more).

Again, our overview of learners in the Learning Landscape reveals that the ability to learn, to move through the Learning Landscape and climb the highest peaks is not about who a person is. It is related to what the person does and the equipment they carry.

GUIDES

Most learners are not alone. They often have guides who show them where to go and how to get there.

Children are often gathered into groups (classes) with a guide (teacher) to show them the way. Adult learners call on coaches and mentors.

Interestingly, the learners who achieve the most, who climb higher and move faster, are guided by people who not only point the way but who also help them fil their backpack. The best guide equips learners for the journey.

SIMILARITIES

As we look even closer at the Learning Landscape, something more profound becomes obvious. All learners are, essentially, the same as each other!

Obviously, all learners are individuals, but in the ways that matter the most in the Learning Landscape, they are the same. Recall that learning takes place by moving. When we look at learners in the Learning Landscape, there's nothing inherent about that learner that makes them significantly more able to move through the Learning Landscape than another. There are no taller, more athletic learners. There are none with an extra set of arms to make climbing easier. There are no learners who are significantly faster, stronger, more flexible or in any other way naturally better able to move through the Learning Landscape.

THE LEARNING LANDSCAPE

Likewise, there are no learners more suited to one part of the Learning Landscape than another. No-one is born significantly more artistic, mathematical or communicative than anyone else.

The stunning conclusion is that the type of learner a person is, how much of the Learning Landscape they explore and how high they climb, is not about who they are, it's about what they do. It's about learners developing their ability to move through the Learning Landscape, increasing their Learner Agency and becoming better learners.

As we'll discuss, anyone can become a better learner. Anyone can become the person who is able to climb the highest peaks or roam far and wide in the Learning Landscape. No-one is naturally better or more capable than anyone else. But that does not mean learners remain that way.

And, of course, circumstance and opportunity influence a learner's learning journey, and, ultimately, where they end up. But if a learner is to get anywhere in the Learning Landscape, if they are to follow a path of their choosing, they must become highly effective learners. The remainder of this book explores how to increase Learner Agency and create better learners, starting with looking at the six fundamentally different learner types in the next chapter.

ABOVE-THE-LINE AND BELOW-THE-LINE LEARNERS

There is no doubt that some learners are more effective than others. They use their time and energy to roam more freely across the Learning Landscape, climbing mountains as well as uncovering more of the Learning Landscape than other learners.

Ultimately, the best learners will have the most choice in life. They can choose the path they take through the Learning Landscape. They embrace opportunities, respond to needs as they arise, take on challenges and face adversities that may not have been part of their intended journey, but must be confronted.

Being a more effective learner is not the result of innate ability. More effective learners adopt a set of behaviours that allow them to explore the Learning Landscape more successfully. They carry with them a backpack full of learning dispositions that they have collected and developed. They access and apply these as they confront challenges. In short, it is what learners *do* that makes them a better learner, not *who they are*.

CHAPTER 2: LEARNERS

As we begin our exploration of the different types of learners, it's useful to identify the learners who stretch themselves to become more than they are today. We call these learners "Above-the-Line Learners". In contrast, learners who seek comfort and do what they can do easily without risk of failure are "Below-the-Line Learners".

ABOVE AND BELOW-THE-LINE LEARNING

Recall that in the Learning Landscape height represents the level of difficulty or complexity of the content being learned. The higher up the mountain a learner ventures, the more complex the content becomes. More foundational content is in the foothills. This level of difficulty, which we can think of as our standards, is represented by contour lines on the Learning Landscape. (See *Chapter 1: The Learning Landscape*)

Most learners, at one time or another, experience learning like this (see Figure 1: The Learning Plateau.). When they start their learning journey, progress comes reasonably easily. They move through the easy content in the lowlands with little difficulty. Then, they enter a phase where progress slows and becomes more difficult. They begin to struggle. They see less gain for their efforts until eventually, progress stops. At this point, learners have reached their "Learning Plateau".

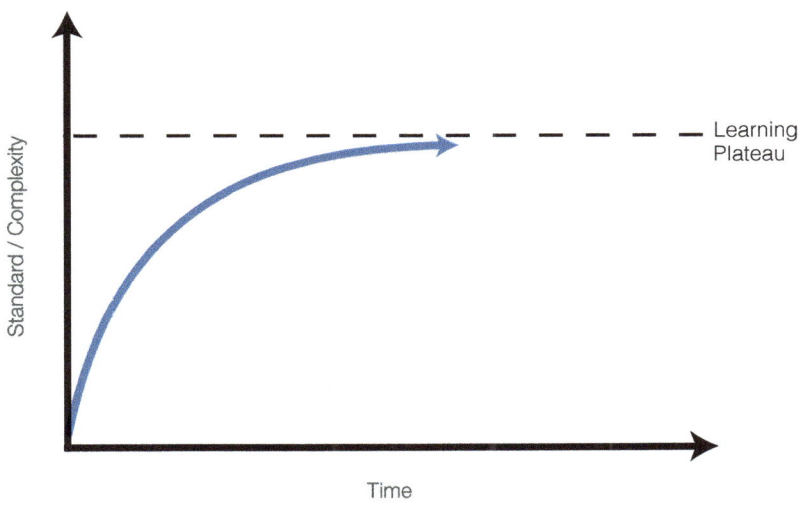

Figure 1: The Learning Plateau.

Source: *The Agile Learner: Where Growth Mindset, Habits of Mind and Practice Unite.*
By James Anderson. Melbourne, VIC: Hawker Brownlow Education © 2017. Reproduced with Permission.

The Learning Plateau represents a person's highest level of achievement. They struggle to move beyond this point, which is marked by a particular contour line. This line represents the best of their (current) ability. We often refer to this level of difficulty as "the bar" (as in, "raise the bar" and improve performance). In the context of the Learning Landscape, we refer to it simply as "the line".

THE LEARNING LANDSCAPE

For Performance Learners, Beginning Learners and Non-Learners, the line takes on a special significance. To them, it represents a permanent limit to their abilities. These learners see everything above this line as beyond their ability. They consider themselves incapable of going higher. They believe that today's best will be tomorrow's best, that their ability to climb is fixed. As a result, they believe any improvement is limited to doing more, not better.

These learners "know", often from experience (see *Chapter 6: Mindset*), that when they attempt tasks above the line, they will fail. They have developed a kind of learned failure. As a result of their fear of failure, they resign themselves to only attempt tasks below the line. They become Below-the-Line Learners.

Below the line feels safe to these learners. They are confident that any learning here will be relatively easy as it's within their current abilities. This area is so easy and comfortable that it is often referred to as the Comfort Zone. Non-Learners and Beginning Learners spend as much of their time as possible in the Comfort Zone (see Figure 2: Comfort Zone. Performance Zone. Learning Zone.).

Performance Learners are a little different. They are still Below-the-line Learners but could be better described as "*Just* Below-the-Line Learners". These learners like to do their best. They like to work on the edge of their abilities where they perform well and make as few errors as possible. Performance Learners like to know they'll get it right, so they avoid trying something they might struggle with and get wrong. This area just below the line is called the Performance Zone.

The problem with Below-the-Line learners is that they never truly grow. Their best never gets better. They become trapped below the line. The challenges beyond their abilities today will remain beyond their abilities tomorrow. Fundamentally, these learners have failed to understand two key ideas: firstly, they have confused learning more with learning better, and secondly, they have misunderstood the true meaning of success.

MORE VERSUS BETTER

BELOW THE LINE - MORE

Below-the-Line Learners confuse learning more with learning better. When they spend time below the line, they still learn new things; they explore and uncover more land in the Learning Landscape. They feel like they are learning because they are covering more ground in the Learning Landscape. But they don't learn more difficult things. They don't climb any higher.

CHAPTER 2: LEARNERS

Learners acquire new knowledge and understandings as their learning journey takes them through the Learning Landscape. As they climb higher, the land below them becomes their Comfort Zone. These lowlands represent a level of difficulty the learner has surpassed; it's below their line.

But just because a learner has climbed to a certain level does not mean they have learned everything in their Comfort Zone. Their learning journey gives them *specific* knowledge and understandings, not *all* knowledge and understandings.

For example, most adults have completed at least some high school-level mathematics. Their learning journey covered their times tables (up to 12), then led them to learn long multiplication, algebra and more complex and difficult mathematics. Most people, having learned up to their 12 times table, don't bother to continue to their 13 times table.

But if an adult wanted to learn their 13 times table, they could easily go back and master it now. As students, they climbed higher than the 13 times table in the Learning Landscape and, although they hadn't explicitly learned it, it is now in their Comfort Zone, below their line.

Knowledge and understandings that are in a learner's Comfort Zone but haven't specifically been learned yet are referred to as "easy things we haven't done yet". The world is full of easy things we haven't done yet. These are tasks we could master easily but haven't taken the time to learn, and might never have the need to learn. As we'll explore in *Chapter 3: Challenges*, these types of challenges, where you learn "easy things you haven't done yet", are called "Downhill Challenges" and, as the name suggests, represent relatively easy learning.

Below-the-Line Learners spend all their time doing "easy things they haven't done yet". They may be active learners, acquiring new knowledge and understandings. They may participate in class and they may be busy. But when they have finished for the day, all they have learned is one more easy thing. They don't learn how to do anything more difficult. They don't become better learners. They have confused learning more with learning better.

Tragically, many people spend their entire adult lives below the line. They stretch and grow at school, and, as a result of being directed to learn (a Directed Learner), they reach a reasonably high level of Learner Agency. This level of ability allows them to spend their lives doing new things – but never anything more difficult. They never truly get better. These people discover that the challenges that were out of their reach when they were 30 remain out of their reach when they are 40, 50, 60 and older. They

THE LEARNING LANDSCAPE

get to the end of their lives and realise, with regret, that they spent their entire adult life doing more, but never getting better.

ABOVE THE LINE – BETTER

Above-the-Line Learners understand the difference between learning more and learning better. They focus their efforts on increasing their Learner Agency and becoming better learners. As a result, the things they are learning tend to be increasingly more difficult, not easy things they haven't done yet.

Above-the-Line Learners include Directed Learners, Independent Learners and Agile Learners. What these learners have in common is that they recognise that "the line" is not a fixed point. It does not define a limit to their abilities; instead, it defines the current extent of their abilities. Beyond the line are challenges that stretch them and demand more of them as learners.

These learners also understand that their "best" is only their best when they measure it by yesterday's standards. They know their best is not a fixed point. By tomorrow's standards, today's "best" will be their second best.

Above-the-Line Learners see the line as a temporary rather than permanent limit. They actively seek to move the line; to raise their level of performance to higher levels by becoming increasingly better learners.

Above-the-Line Learners recognise they aren't *currently* capable of going beyond the line. So, rather than avoid challenges above the line, they work on increasing their abilities so they become more capable of tackling those challenges that are above the line.

The zone just beyond the line is called the Learning Zone. This is the area just beyond a learner's current best and demands slightly more of them than they've been able to apply before. Learners must increase their Learner Agency to go beyond the line and into their Learning Zone. Above-the-Line Learners spend more time in their Learning Zone than Below-the-Line Learners.

How learners can become more capable of meeting the increasingly difficult challenges in their Learning Zone is explored throughout the rest of this book. A key element of this improvement is to continually attempt challenges in their Learning Zone and to try to go beyond their current best. As Anders Ericsson puts it, "It is a fundamental truth ... if you never push yourself beyond your Comfort Zone, you will never improve."[3]

CHAPTER 2: LEARNERS

"Raising the bar" lifts a learner's performance level to new heights. It sees them exploring higher in the Learning Landscape. It also has another profound benefit: it increases the size of a learner's Comfort Zone, expanding the part of the Learning Landscape that includes the "easy things they haven't done yet". We'll explore this idea, along with the essential role a well-stocked backpack has in students becoming better learners, in *Chapter 4: Habits of Mind*.

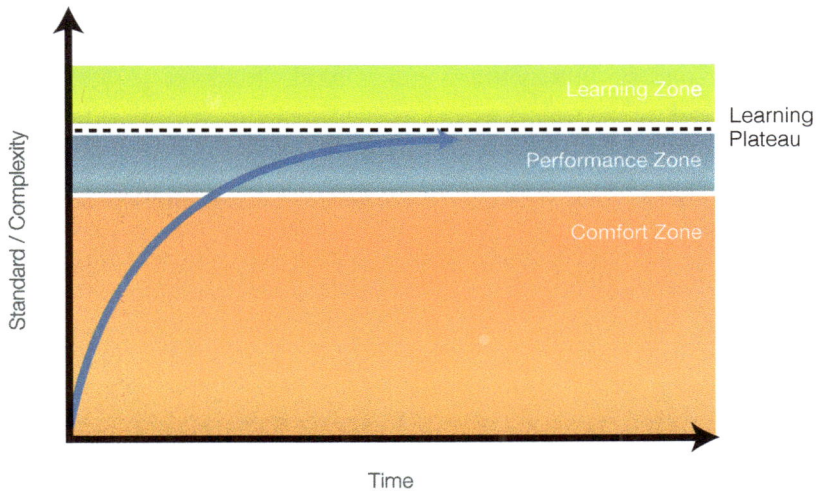

Figure 2: Comfort Zone. Performance Zone. Learning Zone.

Source: *The Agile Learner: Where Growth Mindset, Habits of Mind and Practice Unite.*
By James Anderson. Melbourne, VIC: Hawker Brownlow Education © 2017. Reproduced with Permission.

DEFINING SUCCESS

Both Above-the-Line and Below-the-Line Learners would consider themselves successful. They both learn and acquire new knowledge. The trouble is, they define success differently.

Below-the-Line Learners consider themselves successful when they learn something new. If they finish the day having completed something, having met their goals or able to do something they haven't done before, they consider it a success.

Above-the-Line Learners consider themselves successful only when they learn something more difficult. Success is about raising their standard. These learners aren't happy merely having done more. They aren't content with repeating a performance or standard they've previously achieved. To consider themselves successful, Above-the-Line Learners need to have become better learners and mastered something more difficult. They consider doing the same thing or doing easy things as mostly a waste of time. Their attitude is, "Why do more when you can learn how to do better?"

THE LEARNING LANDSCAPE

In the context of this book, success is defined as achieving a goal above the line. It's not about doing something new and it's not about doing something easy; it's about doing something more difficult.

As we'll discuss in *Chapter 7: Effort*, above-the-line goals require learners to apply "Effective Effort". Effective Effort is more than spending time and energy on a task – both Above- and Below-the-Line Learners do that. It's about how learners spend that time and energy on a task beyond their current best, a task that requires them to raise the bar, to increase Learner Agency and become better learners.

In this way, success isn't about being better than someone else. It's about learners raising their standard and being better than they were yesterday. In *Chapter 6: Mindset* we'll look at professional tennis player Roger Federer, a prime example of someone who understands that success is about improving his game rather than being at any particular standard.

EXPERIENCE VERSUS EXPERTISE

The difference between Above-the-Line and Below-the-Line Learners helps explain why we only find adults on the highest peaks of the Learning Landscape. It also helps explain why not all adults reach the highest peaks. This is the experience versus expertise problem.

To climb to the highest peaks in the Learning Landscape and become an expert takes time. In highly developed fields, such as chess, classical music and some sports, Ericsson points out that reaching a standard that puts learners among the world's best can take up to 10 years of Deliberate Practice.[4]

But it is not time alone that makes someone an expert. It is how they spend that time. If a learner's time is spent below the line, doing more things but never getting better, they will not climb to the highest peaks and become an expert. On the other hand, if a learner spends their time above the line, stretching themselves and developing as a learner, they'll be able to slowly raise the bar of their performance. And when they do that for long enough, they may even become one of the world's best.

This is why we only find adults on the highest peaks of the Learning Landscape, but not all adults reach the peaks. It is not the time on the job, the time spent practising, that counts, it is *how* the time is spent.

CHAPTER 2: LEARNERS

This has important implications for children as they gain an understanding of themselves as learners. Some children (and adults) think their abilities are fixed and that the highest standard they can ever reach in the Learning Landscape is predetermined at birth or by factors beyond their control. These people recognise that they get taller as they get older, and believe in a similar way that any improvement in their abilities that they experience is likewise a result of getting older. This is not true!

Learners don't get better by getting older. They get better because of what they do. This takes time, and people get older as time goes by. If a learner spends their time above the line, their abilities can grow. If they spend their time below the line, their abilities will never improve, and their belief that they will never improve becomes a self-fulfilling prophecy – except they confuse "can't ever get better" with "didn't ever get better".

The difference between the 70-year-old expert and the 70-year-old novice is that the expert spent their life becoming an increasingly good climber. The novice spent their life strolling. Both got older; that happens with time. Expertise happens when you spend that time becoming a better climber.

BACKSTORIES[5]

The difference between Above-the-Line and Below-the-Line Learners highlights another critical aspect of the learner's journey through the Learning Landscape. We each create our own backstory.

Those who reach the highest peaks can overcome the challenges and adversities they encounter in their lives. Their backstory is one of slow, incremental improvement accumulated over a lifetime. As they stand atop the mountain, they can look down over the path travelled and recognise they have come from the lowlands, through the foothills and continued, step by step, to the highest peaks.

As an outsider, it is sometimes easy to look at those who have climbed the highest, those who have succeeded in the most challenging tasks and ignore their backstory. This is particularly true if the first time we see them is when they stand atop a mountain after they have already reached their incredible standards.

We are inclined to celebrate and applaud an expert for *where* they are now. Often, we fail to recognise that they, too, were once in the lowlands. To reach those great heights, they had to spend a lifetime climbing. They were once as we are today, standing in the lowlands, gazing up at the heights, wondering how it would ever be possible for them to climb to the top of those mountains.

THE LEARNING LANDSCAPE

When we recognise and praise these people only for being at the top of the mountain, we do them a great disservice and rob them of their true achievement. As we can see from the stories of Picasso and Mozart (see the end of this chapter), the true achievement is not their highest accomplishment – although that is what we tend to celebrate the most. The true achievement is their backstory of working above the line – of all the small improvements and steps up that mountain that led them to raise their standards and make their greatest achievements possible.

Lao Tzu said, "The journey of a thousand miles begins with a single step," which is true. It is also true that the journey finishes with a single step. It is often the last step we celebrate, but the real achievement is the slow accumulation of each and every step in between.

The critical importance of the backstory has profound implications for what we should value and reward in schools. Real achievement is not the standard a learner is at today – that's temporary. As they achieve higher and higher standards, a learner should be able to look back and recognise that they have been increasing their standard day by day. Too often schools celebrate the standard and ignore or underplay the backstory.

Remember from *Chapter 1: The Learning Landscape*, standards are where the learner is, not who they are. Real achievement is in the backstory that got them there. It comes from increasing Learner Agency, becoming a better learner and consequently improving their standard.

SIX TYPES OF LEARNERS

As we've seen, a student's effectiveness as a learner comes down to what they do, not who they are. It's the actions they take that ultimately create their backstory. Whether it is a backstory of growth and increased ability or whether it is a backstory of sustained mediocrity comes down to Learner Agency and how the student develops as a learner.

Being an Above-the-Line Learner is the first step to becoming an effective learner, but it is *only* the first step.

Learners vary in the way they behave in the Learning Landscape. They adopt different attitudes to challenges (see *Chapter 3: Challenges*), learning behaviours (see *Chapter 4: Habits of Mind*) and the way they engage in the learning process, including the mistakes they make (see *Chapter 5: Practice*). As we'll see in *Chapter 6: Mindset*, these behaviours impact on and are affected by the student's mindset. In *Chapter 7: Effort*,

CHAPTER 2: LEARNERS

we'll look at how each type of learner distributes their time and energy in different ways.

This book is concerned with how students can become better learners. So, we will look at how different learners behave and, importantly, what teachers need to do to help them improve their Learner Agency.

The learner types we'll explore, from highest to lowest Learner Agency, are:
- Agile Learners
- Independent Learners
- Directed Learners
- Performance Learners
- Beginning Learners
- Non-Learners

These categories should not be considered discrete, or in any way permanent, characteristics of the learner. Instead, think of them as a series of recognisable stages in a progression of becoming ever more effective learning. As educators, it's our job to move learners along this progression by teaching them to become more effective learners. Each chapter in this book contains advice and strategies to achieve this.

NON-LEARNERS

These learners are inactive. They fail to take even the most basic steps to explore the Learning Landscape, either above or below the line. As a result, all they do are things they have done before. They uncover no new areas of the Learning Landscape. These learners waste time and fail to engage in any meaningful learning activities.

Because of this, they fail to explore much of the Learning Landscape. You can think of them as spending their time resting comfortably under a tree planted in the lowlands. The rest of their time is spent walking the same well-worn, well-known paths.

THE LEARNING LANDSCAPE

BEGINNING LEARNER

These learners cruise through school. They engage in learning and may appear busy, but they consistently operate below the line. The choose all the easy tasks, the path of least resistance. Although they may learn new things and explore new parts of the Learning Landscape, what they learn is almost exclusively "easy things they haven't done yet".

These learners rarely, if ever, stretch themselves to attempt something more difficult, even when directed by the teacher. They spend as much time as they can get away with in their Comfort Zone and are pushed into their Performance Zone with reluctance. They avoid anything above the line.

Within the Learning Landscape, these students are poorly equipped for learning. They stick to the lowlands, and even then only the well-worn paths.

PERFORMANCE LEARNER

These learners can give the appearance of working hard and being diligent. They continuously strive to do their best, applying themselves to the best of their ability – but not better.

They would prefer to attempt a task that is not challenging and do it very well than attempt a challenging task and risk not doing it well. For these learners, it's largely about looking good. They'd rather be the best player in the B team than the worst player in the A team.

For all their appearance of wanting to do things well, they are still Below-the-Line Learners.

CHAPTER 2: LEARNERS

DIRECTED LEARNER

These learners are often compliant, and will attempt more difficult tasks, stretching themselves above the line, but only when directed to do so. They feel more comfortable below the line.

These learners grow, move through standards and show improvement. But this is largely the result of teacher direction. Without the teacher – their guide in the Learning Landscape – they are likely to retreat below the line and become Performance or Beginning Learners. Of course, this has significant implications for when they are outside a controlled learning environment and there is no-one to push them.

These learners benefit from a directed form of teaching, but teacher instruction needs to go beyond the simple delivery of the curriculum to address the need for them to become better learners.

These learners are focused on doing what the teacher tells them to complete the set task.

INDEPENDENT LEARNER

These learners seek challenges on their own. They are self-directed. They take charge of their learning and set their own above-the-line goals.

These students are beginning to have a deeper understanding of themselves as learners. They can more clearly identify their actions as the cause of their improvement and seek to develop more effective learning behaviours.

In some respects, these learners could be considered selfish. They learn for their own purposes, striking out in their chosen direction through the Learning Landscape. They decide where they want to go and do what they need to get there – and not much else.

THE LEARNING LANDSCAPE

These learners thrive when their goals align with their environment. So, they seek challenges and courses of study – paths through the Learning Landscape – that take them where they want to go.

These Learners may struggle when the learning demands of a situation don't match their chosen goals. For example, they may be Independent Learners in their chosen part of the Learning Landscape, but retreat to being Directed or Performance Learners in other parts that are not to their choosing.

Independent Learners still require guidance and support as they move through the Learning Landscape but benefit from a more coaching style of teaching.

The focus of these learners is on developing their abilities to reach their chosen goals.

AGILE LEARNER

These learners have gone beyond the self-directed, self-centred learning style of the Independent Learner. Rather than choosing their own goals, they are responsive to the demands of the Learning Landscape. Their direction is driven more by circumstance and opportunity than by their own personal agendas.

These students leverage learning opportunities not only to reach new standards but to become better learners. They understand that using a challenge to become a better learner will make future challenges easier to overcome.

These learners are more altruistic in their approach to learning. They take on the challenges that need to be addressed, rather than ones that necessarily meet their own personal agenda. They find purpose and meaning in their learning beyond their own learning needs.

These learners benefit from a more mentoring style of guidance and are focused on achieving goals in order to develop their abilities.

CHAPTER 2: LEARNERS

TEACHER ACTION: DEVELOPING LEARNERS

Reinforce the idea that how much and how well students learn, and how far, wide and high they move through the Learning Landscape, is a result of what they do, not who they are.

Discuss the difference between Above-the-Line and Below-the-Line Learners. Ask students to reflect on the type of learner they might be.

During learning activities, identify when students are expected to learn more (below the line) and when they are learning something more difficult that requires them to become better learners (above the line).

Reflect on the definition of success as "achieving a goal that is above the line". You might like to have a discussion about "successful people". Are these the ones learning more or are these the ones stretching and challenging themselves to learn things that are above the line?

Help students identify where they are in the Learning Landscape today. Over their years of schooling, they have climbed higher but still have a long way to go. Use this to emphasise that all learners, all experts, must climb to the tops of the mountains of expertise – there are no short cuts.

Discuss the experience versus expertise problem. Ask students what they think might be a better use of their time – doing more or doing better?

Use the stories of Mozart and Picasso to reflect on the importance of backstories. Ask students to give examples of people they think "can just do it". Have them investigate these people's backstories to discover when they couldn't "just do it" and highlight the fact that at one stage, these experts were where they are now – in the lowlands.

Learning is a journey and expertise is built as learners slowly climb higher over a long period of time. Ask students what they believe will determine how high a learner will eventually climb as an adult. Is it related to where they are now? Or is it related to what that learner does in the future?

Introduce students to the six different types of learners. Ask them to identify the type of learner they think they are and to identify at least one example of each type of learner, perhaps from the media or stories, etc.

THE LEARNING LANDSCAPE

PICASSO: THE VALUE OF BACKSTORY

There is a story about Spanish artist Pablo Picasso that goes along these lines.

Picasso was sitting on a park bench when a young woman came up to him and asked, "Could you draw me a picture, please?"

Picasso got out his sketchpad and pencil and quickly sketched a portrait of the young woman. She beamed as he handed her the sketch. "Oh, it's so lovely!" she exclaimed.

Before the young woman turned to leave, Picasso said, "That will be one million dollars, please."

"A million dollars!" she said in surprise. "But it only took you two minutes."

"Actually," said Picasso, "it took me a lifetime."

This story highlights the true value of expertise. While we often place value on the end product, the true value of expertise is derived from the years spent developing abilities that make it possible to produce the end product. The real value lies in the backstory.

The backstory is of critical importance in education. Too often, learners ask, "Am I like Picasso?" or, "Do I have the abilities of an Einstein?" They look inside themselves and ask, "What abilities do I have?" They don't expect to have to build their backstory. They expect to just have the abilities.

The notion that we are born with certain talents and abilities is the Fixed Mindset view of the world (see *Chapter 6: Mindset*). Students with a Fixed Mindset expect to "discover" their talents and abilities. They believe people like Picasso have always had their abilities and that's why they can create art. These students believe being an artist comes before doing the art. They don't see the artist's backstory.

CHAPTER 2: LEARNERS

When Picasso states it has taken him a lifetime to produce the drawing, he is crediting his ability to his backstory – a lifetime spent developing his talents. The fact it only took a few moments to create the beautiful sketch is irrelevant. It could not have been created without Picasso's backstory of developing his abilities.

The challenge is that building a backstory of growth is not easy. While many people work at developing their abilities, not everyone does the right sort of work.

It turns out that the Growth Mindset only works when you do the right sort of work! This work can take a lifetime and involves two critical factors:

- *Developing increasingly mature and sophisticated Habits of Mind (see **Chapter 4: Habits of Mind**).*

- *Applying these Habits of Mind just beyond your current best – in your Learning Zone (see **Chapter 3: Challenges**).*

Taken together, the process of developing your Habits of Mind and using them to build expertise creates your backstory. It's your backstory, everything that comes before the achievement, that makes the achievement possible.

Picasso didn't spend a lifetime painting. He spent a lifetime working out how to become a better painter. In the process, he created many paintings, some of which are worth millions of dollars today because they are the reflection of a backstory that created his expertise as a painter.

MOZART: THE HIDDEN BACKSTORY

We have all heard of Wolfgang Amadeus Mozart. Even if we aren't familiar with all his works, we have heard of the legend. A child prodigy who was composing at just six or seven years of age, he was a genius. It's as if his music simply poured out of him, his natural ability unsurpassed by few, if any, other composers.

Mozart was undoubtedly a great musician. His works have stood the test of time, and he is rightly considered by critics to be one of the best classical composers of all time. But were his abilities gifts or were they rewards? Did they come to him innately or were they earned?

In the context of the Learning Landscape, Mozart stood upon the highest peaks in the area of music. His ability to produce and perform beautiful and sophisticated music was comparable to only a few others in history. The question is, how did he get there?

Like Picasso, to understand Mozart's genius, we must dig deep into the legend and look closely at his backstory.

Legend would have it that Mozart was a child genius who was composing at a very early age. While it is true that Mozart composed as a child, it's also misleading. It's easy to assume his compositions as a child were similar to his compositions as an adult. This is not true.

Mozart's celebrated first composition as a child was not a symphony, concerto or opera. It was a 20-second piece for harpsichord. When Mozart composed this piece, he was not an exceptional musician standing atop a mountain in the Learning Landscape. A composition like this is created in the foothills.

In fact, this first piece — admittedly impressive for a young child but not impressive by adult standards — was written in his father's hand, not Mozart's. This brings to light another important aspect of Mozart's backstory — his father.

CHAPTER 2: LEARNERS

Mozart's father, Leopold, was an accomplished musician and professional composer, someone with deep content knowledge of music and composition. As such, he was able to act as a competent guide for Mozart through the Learning Landscape as he developed his skills.

Leopold was not just any guide. He was one of the very few people at the time teaching young children music. In the late 1700s, when Mozart was learning music, most people didn't begin lessons until they were young adults (15–17 years of age). Leopold was teaching young children, including Mozart's sister, how to play music – developing pedagogy and even smaller instruments to fit their small hands. In fact, the book Leopold wrote about how to teach young children music became the seminal work on the subject for the next 100 years.

Clearly, Mozart's guide through the Learning Landscape was not just any old guide, but a highly skilled one who was able to engage Mozart in Deliberate Practice – a type of practice that Anders Ericsson calls the highest and most effective form of practice.[6]

Research from Exeter University suggests that by the time Mozart wrote his first short composition, he may have accumulated as many as 3000 hours of practice – all under the tutelage of an expert musician, composer and teacher.[7] In short, Mozart had already travelled and been guided a long way through the Learning Landscape before he produced his first composition. A composition, incidentally, that was written in his father's hand.

In fact, Mozart didn't create anything that could be described as expert until he was a young adult. His first significant composition, indicating he was standing atop a mountain in the Learning Landscape, wasn't written until he was 21 years old.

Art historians categorise his work up until this time as "loose rearrangements of other people's work".[8] These were not the works of a genius – these were the works of someone learning from other experts. These were works that took place along the road to expertise.

THE LEARNING LANDSCAPE

But in the late 1700s, to see such a young man performing and composing at only 21 years of age was unheard of. Mozart was lauded for his amazing accomplishments at such a young age. The world had never seen such a young man standing atop a mountain of expertise. People could not understand how he could achieve so much so young and assumed he was a natural genius.

But Mozart was not a natural genius. He had toiled through more than 15 years of hard work, under the guidance of an expert teacher, to produce his first significant work. People could not understand how such a young man could compose at such a high level because they did not know Mozart's backstory!

The common backstory for composers at the time was to begin learning music as a young adult. With practice, they would slowly get better and might eventually produce something significant in their early 30s.

The only difference with Mozart's backstory is that he started when he was only five or six years old. He then took 15 years to become an expert – just like other expert musicians, except they tended to start when they were 15–17 years old.

The truth is that to become an expert classical musician, it takes about 15 years of dedicated work under expert guidance. Ericsson would suggest that it requires at least three hours a day of focused attention and Deliberate Practice.[9]

We think we see natural genius only when we see expert performance in the absence of a backstory. Dig a little deeper and it is always the case that the "expert" was a beginner once, and like everyone else, they had to climb to the top of the mountain of expertise.

Expertise is the reward you receive for years of slowly climbing higher and higher in the Learning Landscape. There are no naturals – no-one climbs the mountain of expertise any quicker than anyone else. People only appear to do that if we don't pay attention to their backstory. Real genius is in the backstory.

NASSIM NICHOLAS TALEB: ANTIFRAGILE

Nassim Nicholas Taleb is best described as a modern-day thinker and philosopher. His 2007 book, *The Black Swan: The Impact of the Highly Improbable*, has been described as one of the 12 most influential books since World War II.[10] More recently, his books *Antifragile: Things that Gain from Disorder* (2012) and *Skin in the Game: Hidden Asymmetries in Daily Life* (2018) have been bestsellers. Taleb's work focuses on problems of randomness, probability and uncertainty, which at first glance may seem to have little to do with the Learning Landscape.

Taleb describes systems that are antifragile. Fragile systems break when they are disturbed. Antifragile systems benefit and thrive in disruption. Disruption makes them stronger. Nassim points out that uncertainties, which are an inherent part of the world, make it impossible to predict the future – not just difficult, actually impossible.[11] But while we can't predict the future, we can prepare for it.

The learners of today are growing up in a world that is becoming increasingly uncertain and changeable. The only certainty is change, but there's little certainty about what that change will be! Current thinking in education is that the best way to prepare for this uncertainty is to help learners become robust or resilient. The problem is that robust learners can only resist change. Resilient learners can only recover and return to their original state following disruption. In a rapidly changing world, this isn't good enough.

The world needs learners who are antifragile. These are learners who don't simply withstand or recover from disruption, they embrace it, learn from it and ultimately benefit from the disruption. Taleb's contribution to the Learning Landscape is to help us understand the concept of antifragile. We need to raise our sights beyond resilience and develop learners who will thrive and benefit in an increasingly changing and uncertain world – learners who are antifragile.

Antifragile learners have a deep understanding of themselves as learners. They recognise the nature of different challenges and the need to prepare for the unknowable by developing powerful Habits of Mind. Antifragile learners prepare for an unpredictable future by increasing their Learner Agency and becoming expert learners.

CHAPTER 3
CHALLENGES

Up until now, we've discussed learning in the Learning Landscape as if it was a matter of moving easily from one place to another, acquiring knowledge and understandings along the way. Of course, this is not the case.

Learning something new presents the learner with a challenge. They must move through the Learning Landscape expending time and energy. But not all challenges are equal.

Fundamentally, there are four different types of challenges in the Learning Landscape:

- Downhill Challenges: those that ask nothing more of a learner than what they've achieved before.
- Performance Challenges: those that require a performance equal to a learner's previous best.
- Learning Challenges: those that demand learners stretch slightly beyond their current best and grow to succeed.
- Aspirational Challenges: those that are so far beyond a learner's current ability, they are impossible to master in one step.

In the Learning Landscape, each type of challenge is represented by a different type of "pit". Collectively, we'll refer to these pits as Challenge Pits. The nature of the challenge is determined by the relative heights of the Near Side and the Far Side of the pit.

THE LEARNING LANDSCAPE

NEAR SIDE AND FAR SIDE

A Challenge Pit has two sides: the Near Side and the Far Side (see Figure 3: The Challenge Pit – Near Side and Far Side.).

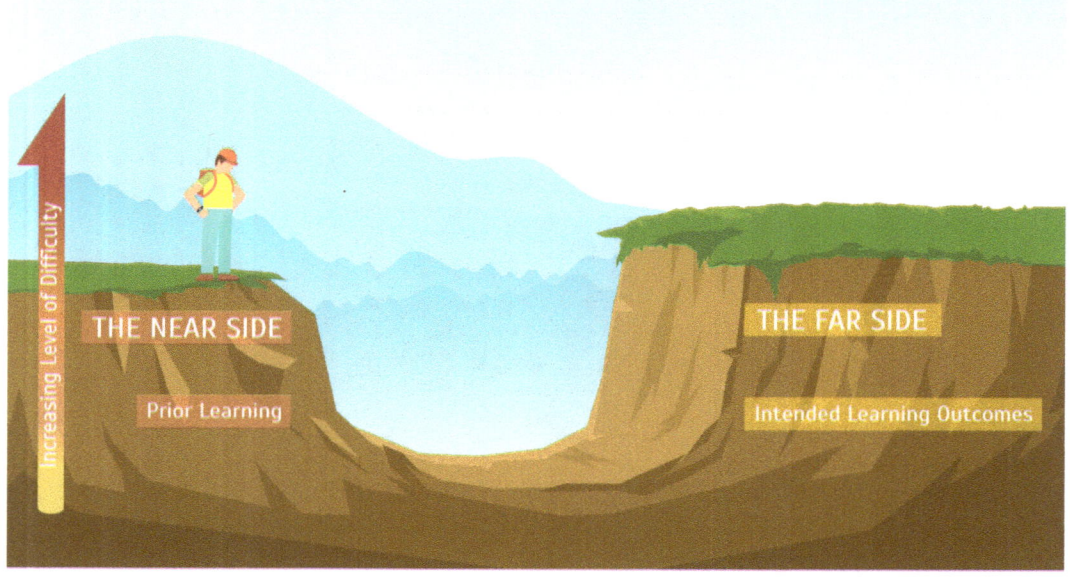

Figure 3: The Challenge Pit – Near Side and Far Side.

THE NEAR SIDE

Recall that learners acquire new knowledge and understanding as they move through the Learning Landscape. Also, as they climb higher, that knowledge and understanding become more complex and difficult. In this way, the Near Side of the Challenge Pit represents all the learner's prior knowledge and understandings.

As the learner approaches a Challenge Pit, we can think of their prior learning as the "earth that's passed beneath their feet". This is everything they've already gained in the Learning Landscape.

If a learner has spent a lot of time "below the line", they may have covered a lot of ground, roaming far and wide in the Learning Landscape, but not have gained much height. They might have "covered a lot of ground" but do not have much "earth beneath their feet".

CHAPTER 3: CHALLENGES

On the other hand, if the learner has spent their time above the line, they would have gained more depth of knowledge and understanding. They've begun their journey up the mountains and are on their way to becoming an expert. With increasing depth and complexity of understanding, the learner has gained mastery over the more difficult aspects of at least one area of the Learning Landscape.

As the learner stands on the Near Side of a Challenge Pit, their most foundational knowledge and understandings are represented by the deepest layers beneath their feet. The more complex, difficult and newly acquired knowledge is near the top.

This is why expertise in an area can be seen as standing on top of a mountain. An expert has successfully climbed through the Learning Landscape, gaining not just more knowledge and understanding, but more complex and demanding knowledge and understandings. They stand atop a mountain of increasingly complex prior learnings.

On the other hand, a beginner has less prior knowledge. What they know and understand is less complex and difficult. They are yet to acquire the deep understandings of an expert. They stand lower in the Learning Landscape.

THE FAR SIDE

The Far Side of the Challenge Pit represents the desired outcome of learning. It is everything to be learned; all the new knowledge and understandings the learner is to acquire and demonstrate during their journey through a Challenge Pit.

The Far Side of the Challenge Pit is often defined by the teacher and/or the needs of the curriculum. It represents the intended learning outcomes being addressed. It is the area of the Learning Landscape yet to be uncovered by the learner. In this way, teachers usually define the Far Side of the Challenge Pit.

Taken together, the Near Side and the Far Side determine the shape of a Challenge Pit and, therefore, the nature of the challenge.

TYPES OF CHALLENGES

Learning is challenging. It takes time and energy to travel through the Learning Landscape, but not all challenges are made equal. Some challenges – and, therefore, Challenge Pits – are easier than others.

THE LEARNING LANDSCAPE

The learner enters a Challenge Pit at their current highest standard, with all their prior knowledge and understanding beneath their feet. They also carry all the learning dispositions they've acquired and developed in their backpack (see *Chapter 4: Habits of Mind*).

Directly below the learner's feet is their Performance Zone. As discussed, this zone represents the highest standard they've previously achieved, having applied the learning dispositions in their backpack. It is their current best.

Below their Performance Zone is their Comfort Zone. This represents all the knowledge and skills they've mastered. This zone also contains the "easy things they haven't done yet".

Slightly above the level they enter a Challenge Pit is their Learning Zone. This represents the next, more difficult step in their learning (see Figure 4: The Challenge Pit – Zones.).

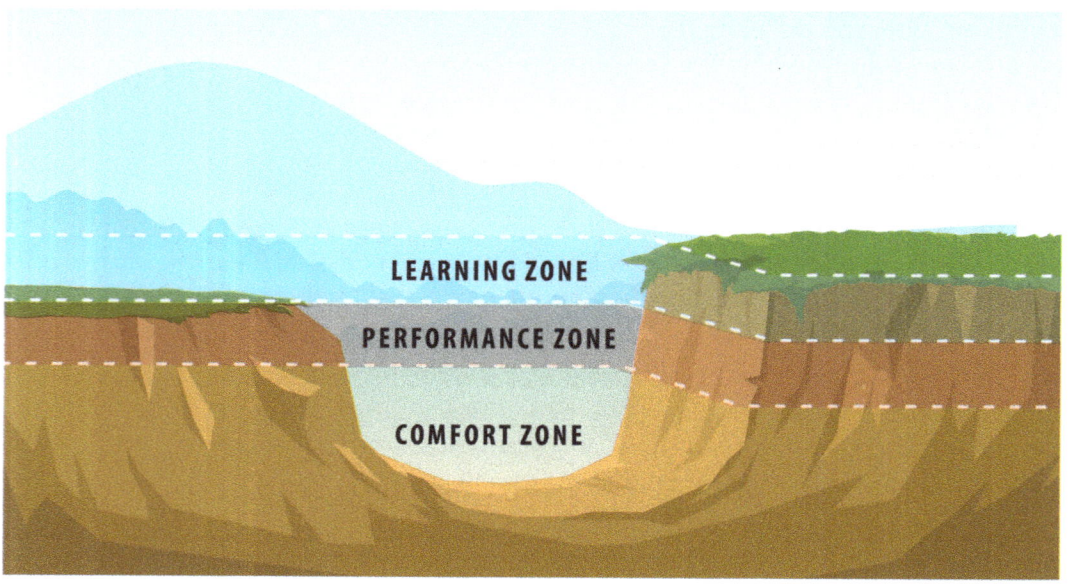

Figure 4: The Challenge Pit – Zones.

HOW CHALLENGING IS A CHALLENGE PIT?

The level of challenge a task presents to a learner is determined by two factors:
1. The "shape" of the Challenge Pit.
2. What's in the learner's backpack.

CHAPTER 3: CHALLENGES

The difference in height between the Near Side and the Far Side of a Challenge Pit determines the type of challenge the learner faces. As introduced earlier, there are four types of challenge: Downhill Challenge, Performance Challenge, Learning Challenge and Aspirational Challenge.

DOWNHILL CHALLENGE

When the Near Side of a Challenge Pit is higher than the Far Side, learners face a Downhill Challenge (see Figure 5: Downhill Challenge.). As you might expect, a Downhill Challenge is not particularly challenging. It asks nothing more of the student than what they have previously achieved. The new knowledge acquired will be less complex than what they've acquired before. Although the student will be learning something new, it will be an "easy thing they haven't done yet". In this situation, the student exits the Challenge Pit via their Comfort Zone.

Because the learning is less complex and less difficult than the learner has previously achieved, the climb out of the Challenge Pit requires no new climbing skills. The learner can call upon a subset of their existing learning behaviours and easily climb out of the pit.

Figure 5: Downhill Challenge.

THE LEARNING LANDSCAPE

PERFORMANCE CHALLENGE

When the Near and Far Sides are the same height, the learner confronts a Performance Challenge (see Figure 6: Performance Challenge.). The level of complexity and difficulty of the knowledge and understandings being learned matches the highest level the learner has previously achieved.

In this case, the learner will need to draw upon their full repertoire of climbing skills to match their previous level of performance.

This student produces their best work, but it is the same "best" as they have produced before, no better. For example, if the student is writing a creative story, it will be different from the stories they've previously written, but it will be of the same standard.

In this sort of challenge, the student exits the Challenge Pit through their Performance Zone. They are doing their best, utilising the maximum of their learning behaviours, but they are not going any further.

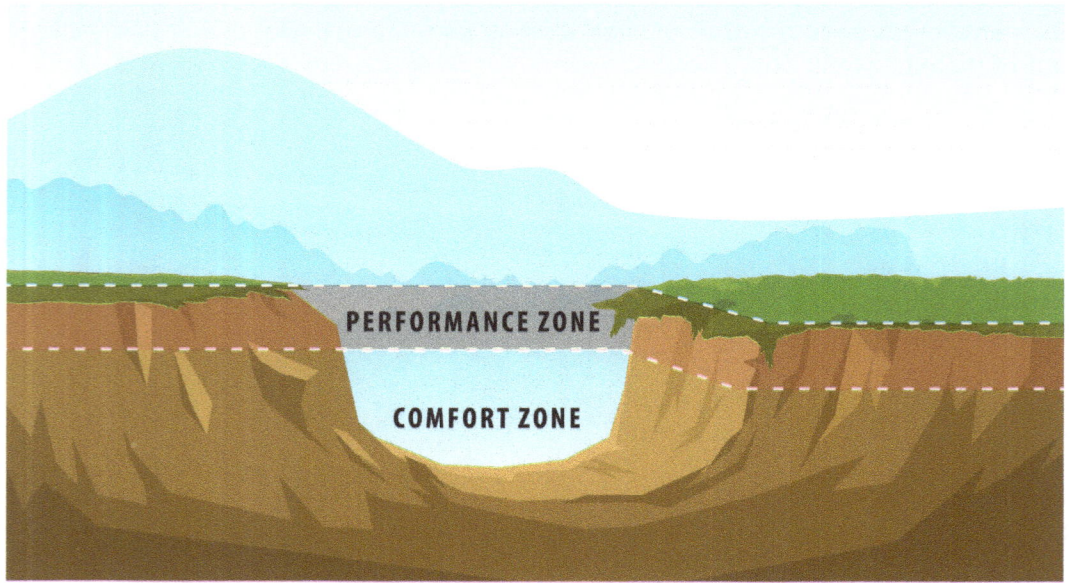

Figure 6: Performance Challenge.

LEARNING CHALLENGE

When the Far Side of the Challenge Pit is *slightly* higher than the Near Side, the student confronts a Learning Challenge (see Figure 7: Learning Challenge.). Ultimately, this is the sort of challenge we want learners to engage in most of the time. It stretches the learner, asking slightly more of them than they've demonstrated in the past.

CHAPTER 3: CHALLENGES

The extra bit of height gained by exiting a Challenge Pit slightly higher than the student entered represents their Learning Zone. The Learning Zone is where they are stretched just beyond their current abilities. This sort of challenge is slightly more difficult than what they've faced before. The knowledge and understandings the learner is trying to gain are more difficult and complex. Succeeding in a Learning Challenge results in the learner gaining more height in the Learning Landscape.

Importantly, when encountering a Challenge Pit, the learner does not usually possess the necessary climbing skills (learning dispositions) required to climb out and acquire this new, more challenging knowledge and understanding. Their current climbing skills only enable them to climb to the same height as the Near Side of the Challenge Pit.

To succeed at a Learning Challenge and come out of the Challenge Pit at a higher, more difficult level, learners must develop new climbing skills. This is the focus of *Chapter 4: Habits of Mind*.

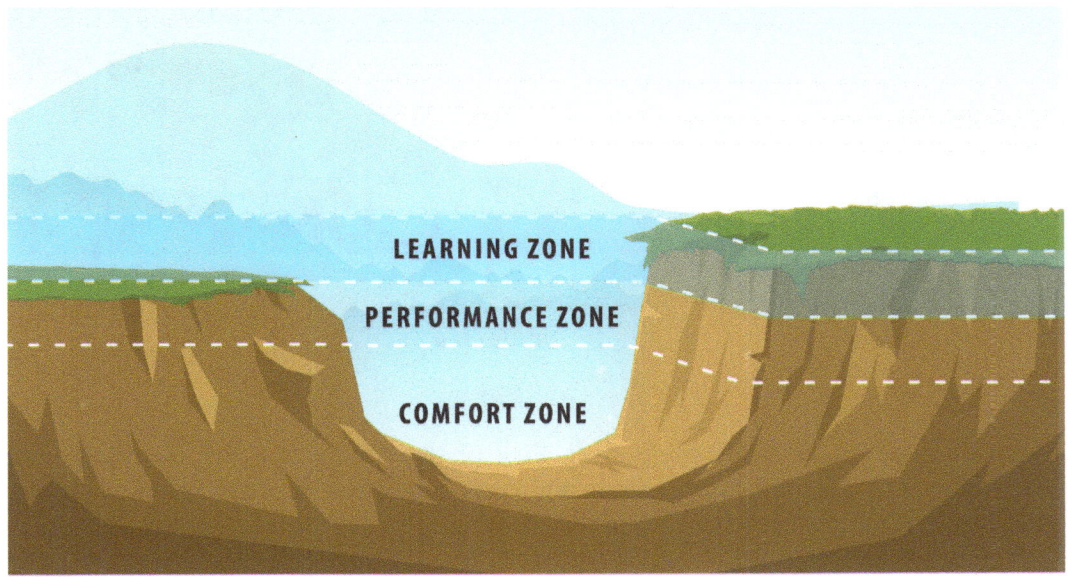

Figure 7: Learning Challenge.

ASPIRATIONAL CHALLENGE

Some challenges are too much to achieve in one go. When the difference between the Near Side and the Far Side of the Challenge Pit is too great, the challenge becomes Aspirational (see Figure 8: Aspirational Challenge.). It is too big to overcome in one attempt, no matter how much time and energy a student expends. This sort of challenge inevitably leads the student to struggle and fail. To overcome an Aspirational Challenge, the task must be broken down into several smaller, but incrementally more difficult, Learning Challenges.

This is not the same as breaking a large task into many little tasks. The point of converting an Aspirational Challenge into smaller Learning Challenges is that each challenge requires slightly more of the learner. They must climb slightly higher with each smaller challenge. A task that is simply large and can be broken into many smaller Downhill or Performance Challenges does not result in an overall improvement.

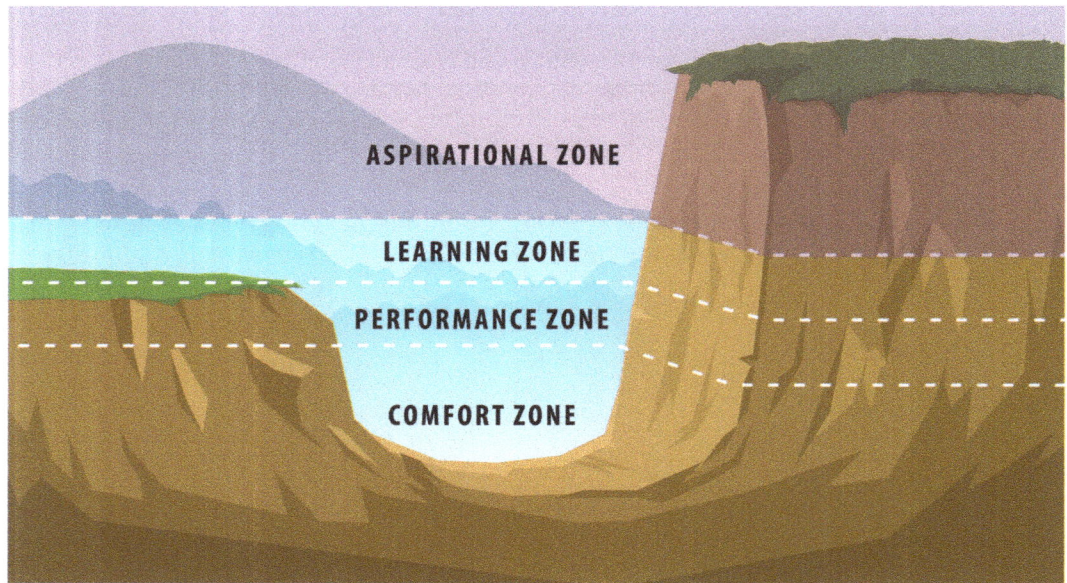

Figure 8: Aspirational Challenge.

SETTING THE RIGHT LEVEL OF CHALLENGE

Teachers usually have a relatively clear view of the Far Side of the Challenge Pit. When we set a task, we often have a full comprehension of what knowledge and understandings are to be acquired and the learning behaviours the challenge demands.

But the difficulty for teachers is that it's not always easy to know what the Near Side – prior knowledge and understandings – of a Challenge Pit looks like for each learner.

Although good teachers always seek to determine a student's prior learning (the ground the learner stands on), it is not always easy to ascertain. The Near Side of the Challenge Pit can be clouded from the teacher's view, obscuring gaps in student understanding and/or insufficiently developed learning behaviours. Furthermore, with 20 or more learners in a classroom, each learner is likely to enter the Challenge Pit at a slightly different height.

CHAPTER 3: CHALLENGES

This has a profound effect on student learning. Although each student might be working on the same task, it could represent a very different type of challenge for each student. A Learning Challenge for one student might be a Downhill Challenge for another. A Performance Challenge for one student might be an Aspirational Challenge for another (see Figure 9: Different Learners Experience the Same Task Differently.).

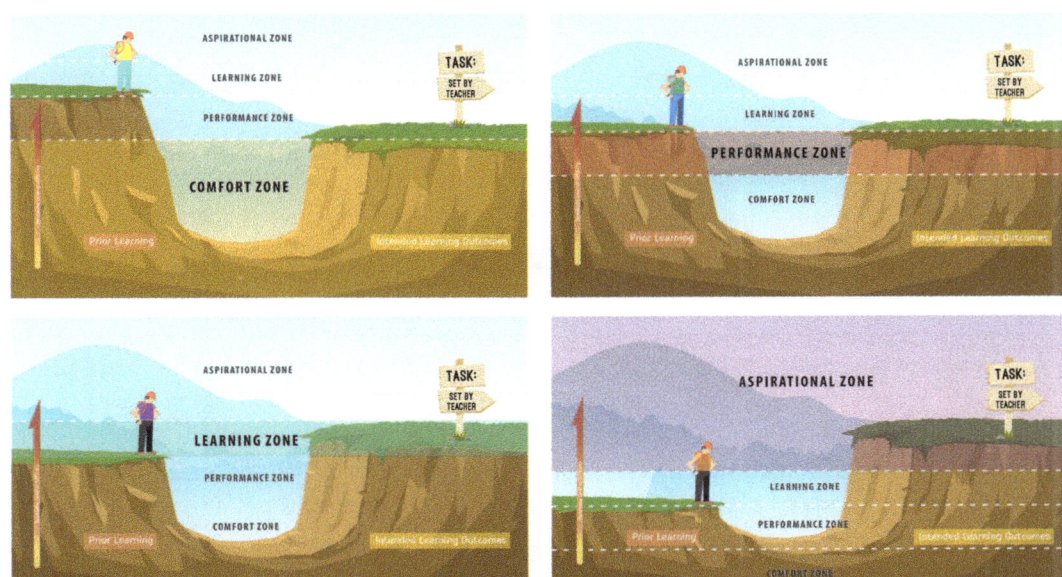

Figure 9: Different Learners Experience the Same Task Differently.

Teachers must ensure every student is appropriately challenged. This means they must consider what the Near Side of the Challenge Pit looks like for each learner and ensure that learning tasks represent Learning Challenges for each student.

This is what differentiation looks like in the Learning Landscape. It's about differentiating based on what learners can bring to the task – their prior learning (the ground beneath their feet) – and what Learning Dispositions (Habits of Mind) are in their backpack. Teachers differentiate so they can appropriately challenge students and develop their Learner Agency so every student can become a better learner.

It is important to recognise that we are not differentiating based on the learner. Rather, we are differentiating based on what the learner brings to the Learning Challenge.

Fortunately, the Learning Zone is a relatively wide area, and students with similar levels of prior knowledge and skills are likely to all exit a Challenge Pit through their Learning Zone for the same task.

THE LEARNING LANDSCAPE

LEARNING CHALLENGES ARE ALWAYS CHALLENGING

Learning Challenges demand concentration, time, energy and the right sort of effort. It does not matter what specific content is to be gained, what part of the Learning Landscape needs to be explored or at what height the Learning Challenge takes place. A learner will always find an appropriate Learning Challenge challenging.

What makes a Learning Challenge challenging is the relative difference between the Near Side and the Far Side of the Challenge Pit. It is the extra bit of height gained. This extra height also demands new climbing skills. It is these two factors – the change in height and the need for new climbing skills – that represent the "challenge". This is of critical importance: the challenge in learning lies in the *change* of standard, not the standard itself.

For example, if we asked an 8-year-old and a 30-year-old to do the same novel task, the task would be "new" to both. But the 30-year-old would likely bring far more prior knowledge and understandings, as well as more sophisticated learning behaviours, to the task. What might be a Learning Challenge or even an Aspirational Challenge for the 8-year-old would likely be a Downhill Challenge for the 30-year-old. In this way, the amount of "challenge" lies in the change of standard and what's in the learner's backpack, not the standard itself.

This has two significant consequences. Firstly, learning; real learning – uphill learning, that stretches students, helps them grow and gains them height in the Learning Landscape – will always take effort for *every* learner – regardless of whether they are a novice or an expert. Gaining height in the Learning Landscape is challenging.

Teachers and learners need to be aware of this fact. The standard does not set the level of the challenge. The challenge comes from two factors:

1. The change in height (standard) between the Near Side and Far Side of the Challenge Pit. Therefore, teachers cannot set challenging tasks without first considering the learner's prior knowledge and the learning dispositions they bring to the task.
2. How well prepared the learner is for the climb. This relates to how full their backpack is, which we will explore in *Chapter 4: Habits of Mind*.

This means, for example, that high school should not be more (or less) challenging for the learner than primary school. Certainly, the standards will be different. The learning outcomes attempted in secondary school will be more difficult and complex. But the level of challenge experienced by the student is determined by the amount of growth – the change of standard – that is required, not the standard itself.

CHAPTER 3: CHALLENGES

THE REAL BENEFIT OF CLIMBING

There are three benefits to taking on Learning Challenges.

The first and most immediate is that learners gain height in the Learning Landscape. They acquire new and more difficult knowledge and understandings and are likely to complete the task at hand. These new learnings can then be applied in life. This has the benefit of helping learners to achieve more highly, leading them to gain even greater expertise in an area.

Secondly, as learners climb higher in the Learning Landscape, more and more of the challenges they encounter are Downhill Challenges. They effectively expand their Comfort Zone, making more of the Learning Landscape "easy things they haven't done yet". This is, of course, in contrast with Below-the-Line Learners, who spend their lives doing more but not getting better. For Below-the-Line Learners, some challenges will remain forever out of reach in their Aspirational Zone. On the other hand, as Above-the-Line Learners climb the heights of the Learning Landscape, more and more challenges fall within their abilities.

Finally, to climb higher, students must become better learners. They must fill their backpack with new learning strategies. This increases their Learner Agency and makes them better learners.

How to fill a learner's backpack, and what to fill it with, is the focus of *Chapter 4: Habits of Mind*.

HOW DIFFERENT LEARNERS RELATE TO THEIR LEARNING ZONE

The most effective learners understand that learning is meant to be challenging and, ultimately, it's the challenge that helps them grow.

NON-LEARNERS

Non-Learners **avoid** their Learning Zone. In fact, they avoid any sort of challenge at all. They would prefer to do nothing than take on a challenging task.

THE LEARNING LANDSCAPE

BEGINNING LEARNERS

Beginning Learners **reduce** the level of challenge in a task. When given the opportunity, they take the easiest path, seeking to work in their Comfort Zone.

PERFORMANCE LEARNERS

Performance Learners **limit** the challenges they face. They are prepared to do their best, but not to attempt better than their best. They seek tasks they know they can do well. These tasks are in their Performance Zone. They focus on things they have done well before and repeat that performance, or perform similar tasks they are confident are within their abilities.

All Below-the-Line Learners, including Beginning Learners and Performance Learners, are vulnerable. Their reliance on their current abilities, without an understanding of how to increase those abilities, puts them at risk of finding themselves in circumstances they can't cope with. The challenges and adversities they encounter will frequently be Aspirational Challenges that remain out of their reach.

DIRECTED LEARNERS

Directed Learners **attempt** tasks in their Learning Zone upon the direction of the teacher. As a result, Directed Learners do see improvement and growth in standards. But their reliance on external drivers leaves them in need of structured learning environments that guide their learning. In the absence of structures that identify their Learning Zone for them, they can return to being a Below-the-Line Learner.

Directed Learners are rarely "lifelong" learners. They learn as long they are being directed to do so, then stop. They thrive in environments that give them direction, such as schools, universities and some workplaces. But as soon as this direction ends, they no longer gain height in the Learning Landscape, develop further Learner Agency or fill their backpack.

Directed Learners are fragile. Although they may thrive in a stable environment, if that environment changes, they require outside assistance to respond to it. In the absence of this structured environment, they may find their skills are no longer sufficient.

CHAPTER 3: CHALLENGES

INDEPENDENT LEARNERS

Independent Learners **target** specific goals that meet their needs. They understand the need to stretch themselves into their Learning Zone to reach specific goals. For example, a person might decide they want a promotion at work, so they target and work towards specific goals with the purpose of achieving the promotion.

But having reached their target, there is the risk that the Independent Learner will fall back into their Performance Zone. They may be inclined to demonstrate their newly achieved level of competence without pursuing further growth until a new target becomes necessary. In the above example, the person receives the promotion and performs capably in the new role, but does not choose to continue to learn.

Independent Learners grow as long as their goals remain out of reach. They can be lifelong learners if they continue to set themselves new challenges. In this way, their learning might be viewed as selfish. Their goals are their own. They pursue them at their discretion for their own gains.

Many elite athletes and academics are Independent Learners. They set their own goals and push themselves to perform at higher and higher levels. Athletes constantly try to perform "better" than before. Their goal is one of continual improvement. Likewise, academics continually look for new problems they want to solve, the next challenge in their field.

Independent Learners are resilient. They can respond to challenges by targeting new learning. But this is a responsive measure that may come too late or too slowly. When adversity and unforeseen difficulties strike, Independent Learners may find themselves ill-equipped to deal with these changes.

Remember, a challenge is a gap between where the learner is and where the learner *wants* to be. It's something the learner chooses. Adversity is the gap between where the learner is and where they *need* to be. It's something forced on them by circumstance, something they don't have a choice in.

AGILE LEARNERS

Agile Learners **embrace** challenges of all types. They are responsive to the needs of their environment and use challenges to increase their Learner Agency.

THE LEARNING LANDSCAPE

They know that continually taking on all types of challenges helps them become better learners. This is how they reach new heights in the Learning Landscape, ensuring more and more future challenges become "easy things they haven't done yet". They are in the business of constant growth and are true lifelong learners.

Agile Learners are less selfish and more selfless in their learning. They confront the challenges that are the most pressing in the environment they are in. Unlike the Independent Learner, who has a personal agenda of reaching specific goals, the Agile Learner's only agenda is to become a better learner – so they are better equipped to succeed when confronted with adversities or challenges.

Agile Learners are also antifragile (see the description of Nassim Nicholas Taleb's "Antifragile" in the following section). They thrive in an environment that is volatile, uncertain, changeable and ambiguous. Constant adversity gives them the fuel they need to grow as learners and, as they grow, they become more and more capable, equipping themselves increasingly well to confront the next unforeseen challenge.

ANTIFRAGILE

Everyone understands what it means when something is fragile. When you disturb something fragile, it breaks. We wrap fragile things in special packaging to protect them from shocks and stick on a label that says, "Handle with care."

What, then, is antifragile?

Many people assume that the opposite of fragile is strong, robust or resilient. This isn't the case. Things that are strong or robust simply resist disturbances. We can drop them and they won't break. Things that are resilient "bounce back" to their initial state. After they are disturbed, they recover and return to what they were before.

But things that are antifragile benefit from disruption. Instead of breaking, resisting or recovering when they are disturbed, they grow. We'd wrap things that are antifragile in packaging that says, "Please handle without care," and, "Please drop frequently to improve quality."

Author Nassim Nicholas Taleb explores the concept of things that are antifragile in his book of the same name. He uses a shrub as a basic example. Left to grow on its own, a shrub tends to develop into a sparsely leaved plant. Given a good prune every so often, it responds with extra shoots and thrives. It benefits from the disturbance.

CHAPTER 3: CHALLENGES

Taleb points out that although we've previously lacked a word for it, antifragility is inherent in the systems that endure. Evolution is an antifragile system. Small changes and challenges in the environment constantly weed out the weakest links, improving the system as a whole. There are many other examples of these systems.

Antifragility has special significance to our discussion about different types of learners. Today's learners will be growing up in a VUCA world – one that is Volatile, Uncertain, Changeable and Ambiguous. It is changing rapidly and unpredictable. As a result, learners will be subject to more disruptions than previous generations. Taleb points out that while it is impossible to predict the future, we can prepare for it. We can prepare for this uncertain future by creating systems – and, in our case, learners – that thrive on disruption.

Disruption has the effect of pushing learners out of their Comfort Zone and into their Learning Zone. When we develop learners who know how to behave in their Learning Zone – who can respond to a challenge or adversity and use it to help them grow – we create learners who will thrive in the world of the future.

Unfortunately, much of the discussion in education focuses on building resilient learners. The literature, for example, talks about protective factors and bouncing back. This focus sets the bar too low for learners who will be in a highly unpredictable and changeable world. Rather than teaching students to recover from setbacks, we need to teach them to embrace and leverage challenges to help them become even better learners. Like the example of the shrub, we don't want learners to merely return to the way they were before the disturbance – we want them to grow as a result! Such learners would be antifragile and thrive in the disruptive world of the future.

TEACHER ACTION: SETTING THE CHALLENGE

Explain the concepts of a Learning Challenge and Challenge Fits to students, including the idea that the Near Side represents all their prior learning and the Far Side represents their new learning.

Distinguish each new challenge as being a Downhill, Performance or Learning Challenge. As the teacher, ensure all students are frequently (but not always) experiencing Learning Challenges.

Help students identify when a challenge is an Aspirational Challenge – this might be something that will be achieved later in the year.

THE LEARNING LANDSCAPE

Ask students to describe how they feel when engaged in different types of challenges. What types of challenges do they prefer? (See *Chapter 6: Mindset*).

Discuss the idea that each Learning Challenge feels "challenging", but they don't get *more* challenging. Help students understand that, like climbing stairs, each step going up is as challenging as the last. They don't need to fear it becoming increasingly challenging.

Develop the language of the Challenge Pits, Comfort Zone, Performance Zone, Learning Zone and Aspirational Zone, and make these terms part of your language for learning in the classroom. Help students identify these zones in their learning.

Ask students to select challenges that put them in their Comfort, Performance or Learning Zones. Help them identify times when it is appropriate to be in each of these zones. This is especially important in goal-setting exercises.

Help students recognise when they have mastered new learning and that things that were once in their Learning Zone are now in their Comfort Zone. They have "raised the bar" and climbed higher in the Learning Landscape. Celebrate this as a success (see *Chapter 2: Learners*).

Describe how different learners respond to the Learning Zone to help students identify the type of learner they are today. What might they need to focus on to become a better learner?

CHAPTER 3: CHALLENGES

ABOUT LEARNING CHALLENGES AND LEARNING PITS™

The idea of using a pit to represent a challenge is not new in education. Others have used a pit to represent what Lev Vygotsky described as the Zone of Proximal Development (also known as the "Learning Zone").[17] These include John Edwards and Bill Martin, and, perhaps most notably, James Nottingham, who draws on Edwards' work in describing the Learning Pit™.[18,19,20] While all these authors, as well as myself, draw upon the analogy of a pit, there are several important distinctions to be made, particularly between my work and the work of James Nottingham.

Firstly, in the Learning Landscape, the vertical axis in the analogy of the pit relates to difficulty, complexity and standards. Going down into the pit accesses foundational knowledge and prior learning and climbing higher results in gaining more complex and difficult understandings, eventually leading to expertise.

The work of Edwards and Nottingham depicts a vertical axis related to confusion/clarity. Going down into the Learning Pit results in cognitive conflict. In Nottingham's work, climbing higher results in clarity of understanding of a concept. While there is a loose similarity here, it is not the same thing.

In the Learning Landscape, a pit represents one of four different types of challenges. Each pit in the Learning Landscape may differ in the relative height of the near side and the far side. In Nottingham's work, there is only one pit and, and when drawn correctly, a Learning Pit™ always has a higher side on the right.

In the Learning Landscape, the Learning Zone is represented by the slight increase in height on the Far Side of the Learning Pit. In Nottingham's work, the Learning Zone is represented by the pit itself. Nottingham's analogy does not depict the Performance Zone or Aspirational Zone, which are of central concern to understanding the learner's journey through the Learning Landscape.

In the Learning Landscape, pits represented by Downhill Challenges and Performance Challenges are incompatible with Nottingham's Learning Pit™. To be in Nottingham's Learning Pit™ and in your Comfort Zone is the opposite of what Nottingham describes.

THE LEARNING LANDSCAPE

In the Learning Landscape, teachers define learning outcomes by establishing the Far Side of the pit. In Nottingham's Learning Pit, the outcomes are almost entirely student driven. As we will discuss in *Chapter 5: Practice*, Ericsson asserts that the learner's ability to clearly define their learning goals is an essential part of building expertise – it tells the learner where they're going in the Learning Landscape.[21]

Nottingham's model includes a four-stage learning process: Concept, Conflict, Construct, Consider. Central to this process is to begin with a concept. Although it would be possible to use a similar pedagogy drawing on the Learning Landscape metaphor, beginning with a concept is not necessary in the Learning Landscape. The way the pit is applied in the Learning Landscape relates equally to concepts as it does to scientific method, throwing a javelin, drawing, improving memory, flying fighter jets or, in fact, any and all learning endeavours.

Further, Nottingham's Learning Challenge is usually depicted as a collaborative exercise, with students getting into the pit together. This is not the case in the Learning Landscape, as the shape of each Challenge Pit is different based on each learner's prior learning. While learners are free to learn collaboratively in the Learning Landscape, the pit relates to the individual's journey. In fact, because the near side of the Challenge Pit is defined by the student's prior learning, for a given task the shape of a Challenge Pit is likely to be different for each individual student.

Importantly, the Learning Landscape represents a clear metaphor for lifelong learning. The journey through the Learning Landscape creates a unique backstory specific to each individual. In the context of the Learning Landscape, a pit is just one of many learning experiences on a journey towards expertise.

ART COSTA AND BENA KALLICK: HABITS OF MIND

Professor Emeritus Art Costa and Dr Bena Kallick are the co-creators and co-authors of the Habits of Mind. Drawing on decades of research by eminent educators, psychologists and others, Costa and Kallick define the dispositions that are skilfully and mindfully engaged by characteristically successful people when confronted with problems, the solutions to which are not immediately apparent.[22]

Costa and Kallick are the directors of the Institute for Habits of Mind and have co-authored and edited numerous books, including *Learning and Leading with Habits of Mind* (2008), *Habits of Mind Across the Curriculum* (2009), *Dispositions: Reframing Teaching and Learning* (2014) and *Assessment Strategies for Self-Directed Learning* (2004).

They describe 16 Habits of Mind (see *Chapter 4: Habits of Mind*). Part of the skilfulness learners develop in applying the Habits of Mind is recognising the contexts in which each should, and should not, be applied. It is not that we want learners to apply all the Habits of Mind all the time. Rather, we want them to become attuned to selecting the Habits of Mind most appropriate to a situation.

The Habits of Mind are dispositions towards a way of action. As such, they cannot be defined by any one action. Each Habit of Mind encompasses a range of skills, tools and strategies. In this way, skilful learners further develop their Habits of Mind by adding to this repertoire of strategies.

In the context of the Learning Landscape, the Habits of Mind define a set of behaviours that, as they are refined and developed, allow learners to continue to move through and climb higher in the Learning Landscape. They are the tools learners put in their backpacks to draw upon to successfully climb out of a Challenge Pit. Highly skilful learners, those with the greatest Learner Agency, have exceptionally well-developed Habits of Mind.

CHAPTER 4
HABITS OF MIND

Setting Learning Challenges is only part of the story. To learn and gain new knowledge and understandings that are part of a Learning Challenge, learners must know how to climb out of the pit. Unfortunately, not all learners can do this and, as a result, some remain stuck at the bottom of the pit, discouraged and unable to succeed.

As educators, it is not enough to simply set an appropriately challenging task. We must *prepare learners for the climb* out of the Challenge Pit. This means we must teach them the learning behaviours – the Habits of Mind – that will aid them in their climb. In the context of this analogy, we must fill learners' backpacks with the learning dispositions that will allow them to climb out. Students stranded at the bottom of a pit simply don't have the learning dispositions they need in their backpack. They are waiting for their teacher to help them fill it!

Too many learners are set challenging tasks but are not adequately prepared to succeed and climb out of a Challenge Pit. As we shall discuss in *Chapter 6: Mindset*, this leads learners to incorrectly believe they will never be able to climb out of a Challenge Pit, and they then fear taking on any challenge.

This chapter will focus on the learning dispositions, or Habits of Mind, learners need to climb out of a Challenge Pit – specifically a Learning Challenge. Here, we will build on and apply the work of Art Costa and Bena Kallick to the Learning Landscape. We describe developing these behaviours as "filling the learner's backpack".

THE LEARNING LANDSCAPE

WHAT GOES IN A BACKPACK?

As we noted in *Chapter 1: The Learning Landscape*, success in the Learning Landscape is related to what you do, not who you are. There are no significant innate qualities that make some people naturally better learners than others. The stories of Mozart and Picasso at the end of *Chapter 2: Learners* highlighted the fact that what makes someone able to perform at a very high standard is not who they are but what they do and their backstory of slow, incremental improvements. These skilful learners acquire a formidable set of learning dispositions that allow them to take on the greatest heights of the Learning Landscape and achieve the highest standards.

In *Chapter 1: The Learning Landscape*, we also recognised that the learners who reach the greatest heights have the largest backpacks. Although all learners are (essentially) the same, the most successful ones are better equipped. They have filled their backpacks with a set of learning dispositions that enable them to take on the most difficult Learning Challenges to reach the peaks of the Learning Landscape.

Costa and Kallick identify these effective learning dispositions as the Habits of Mind. They define these as the dispositions that are skilfully and mindfully employed by characteristically successful people when confronting problems, the solutions to which are not immediately apparent.

In the context of the Learning Landscape, we find problems (to which the solutions are not immediately apparent) in the Learning Zone. By contrast, when we are in our Comfort or Performance zones, the solutions to problems *are* immediately apparent.

Within the analogy of the Learning Landscape, the Habits of Mind are the tools learners store in their backpacks and use to climb out of a Challenge Pit. Importantly, they are the tools that, when well developed, fill the backpacks of the very best climbers as they attempt to climb even higher. They are also the tools missing from the backpacks of learners who struggle and fail to climb out of a Challenge Pit. Therefore, helping struggling learners to succeed is in no small way related to filling their backpacks with well-developed Habits of Mind.

A list of the Habits of Mind, along with their definitions, can be found in Figure 10: Habits of Mind – Costa and Kallick's 16 Habits of Mind.

In the context of the Learning Landscape, the Habits of Mind form a basic toolkit for students as they learn to become better climbers.

CHAPTER 4: HABITS OF MIND

HABITS OF MIND

1. Persisting

 Stick to it! Persevering in task through to completion; remaining focused. Looking for ways to reach your goal when stuck. Not giving up.

2. Managing impulsivity

 Take your Time! Thinking before acting; remaining calm, thoughtful and deliberative.

3. Listening with understanding and empathy

 Understand Others! Devoting mental energy to another person's thoughts and ideas. Make an effort to perceive another's point of view and emotions.

4. Thinking flexibly

 Look at it Another Way! Being able to change perspectives, generate alternatives, consider options.

5. Thinking about your thinking (Metacognition)

 Know your knowing! Being aware of your own thoughts, strategies, feelings and actions and their effects on others.

6. Striving for accuracy

 Check it again! Always doing your best. Setting high standards. Checking and finding ways to improve constantly.

7. Questioning and problem posing

 How do you know? Having a questioning attitude; knowing what data are needed and developing questioning strategies to produce those data. Finding problems to solve.

8. Applying past knowledge to new situations

 Use what you Learn! Accessing prior knowledge; transferring knowledge beyond the situation in which it was learned.

9. Thinking and communicating with clarity and precision

 Be clear! Striving for accurate communication in both written and oral form; avoiding over generalizations, distortions, deletions and exaggerations.

10. Gather data through all senses

 Use your natural pathways! Pay attention to the world around you Gather data through all the senses; taste, touch, smell, hearing and sight.

11. Creating, imagining, and innovating

 Try a different way! Generating new and novel ideas, fluency, originality

12. Responding with wonderment and awe

 Have fun figuring it out! Finding the world awesome, mysterious and being intrigued with phenomena and beauty.

13. Taking responsible risks

 Venture out! Being adventuresome; living on the edge of one's competence. Try new things constantly.

14. Finding Humor

 Laugh a little! Finding the whimsical, incongruous and unexpected. Being able to laugh at oneself.

15. Thinking interdependently

 Work together! Being able to work in and learn from others in reciprocal situations. Team work.

16. Remaining open to continuous learning

 I have so much more to learn! Having humility and pride when admitting we don't know; resisting complacency.

www.jamesanderson.com.au
Source: *Habits of Mind Across the Curriculum: Practical and Creative Strategies for Teachers.*
By Arthur L. Costa and Bena Kallick. Alexandria. VA. ASCD. © 2009. Reproduced with Permission. Visit www.ascd.org

Download this infographic in full size from jamesanderson.com.au/the-learning-landscape-resources

Figure 10: Habits of Mind – Costa and Kallick's 16 Habits of Mind.

THE LEARNING LANDSCAPE

BECOMING A BETTER CLIMBER

The Habits of Mind are not a discrete set of 16 tools. It's not like one is a hammer, one is a saw and another a ruler. These learning dispositions overlap and interact with each other. To be able to "Listen with Empathy and Understanding", you also need to "Think Flexibly", "Manage Impulsivity" and "Strive for Accuracy". But while we do frequently call upon the Habits in groups or clusters, it is also useful to think of them independently.

Further, students can't just collect all 16 Habits of Mind and become the perfect learner! Every learner already has all the Habits of Mind, but what is often lacking is refinement, increased complexity and maturity in the way they are applied.

The Habits of Mind need to be continually developed to help learners climb higher in the Learning Landscape. For example, instead of merely "Persisting", students must learn how to get better at persisting. This does not simply mean persisting more often; it means doing it more skilfully and mindfully. To become better learners, students must learn to apply these dispositions in increasingly sophisticated ways.

Recall that in the Learning Landscape, difficulty and complexity of knowledge and understanding relate to height. Relatively easy tasks are found in the lowlands. As learners climb higher, they encounter increasingly more complex and difficult tasks, which require more well-developed Habits of Mind. Put another way, the higher a learner wants to go in the Learning Landscape, the more they need to fill their backpack to succeed!

To work on relatively easy foundational tasks, a learner's Habits of Mind don't need to be highly developed. That's why you'll find a lot of people with relatively small backpacks in the lowlands of the Learning Landscape. These poorly filled backpacks are quite sufficient in the lowlands. Easy tasks don't require sophisticated Habits of Mind.

As learners climb higher, the tasks become inherently more difficult. As a result, their Habits of Mind must become increasingly well developed. This is why you'll only find very well-equipped learners with large backpacks in the highlands and mountaintops of the Learning Landscape.

For example, holding a conversation with friends requires moderately well-developed Habits – those of "Listening with Empathy" and "Communicating with Clarity and Precision" (plus a few others). If that's all you ever do, your backpack wouldn't need to be very full. But negotiating a peace treaty between warring nations with different belief systems would require these same Habits to be much more highly developed.

CHAPTER 4: HABITS OF MIND

THE BACKPACK AND GETTING OUT OF A PIT

As we discussed in *Chapter 3: Challenges*, the Near Side of a Challenge Pit represents everything a learner brings to a challenge. The earth they stand on is all their prior knowledge and understandings, with the most complex and difficult understandings directly beneath their feet and the simpler, most foundational understandings deeper down.

Learners don't approach a Challenge Pit with their prior knowledge and understandings alone. They also approach it with their backpack full of climbing tools – their Habits of Mind.

As a learner stands on the Near Side of a Learning Challenge, their backpack contains all the Habits of Mind that have enabled them to climb to their current standard. If the challenge before them is a Performance Challenge or a Downhill Challenge, then they can be confident that the Habits of Mind in their backpack will be sufficient. These types of challenges ask nothing more difficult of learners than what they've already achieved. People don't need to become better learners to succeed in these sorts of challenges.

But what's in a learner's backpack will be insufficient if the challenge is a Learning Challenge. A Learning Challenge, one that requires the learner to climb higher than they've climbed before and take on a task more difficult than they've previously confronted, demands that they equip themselves with more well-developed Habits of Mind. Without filling their backpack with the skills and tools necessary to succeed at these more difficult tasks, they will fail to climb out of the Learning Challenge pit.

This is why some learners get to a point where they reach what appears to be a permanent Learning Plateau – the point in the Learning Landscape that, to them, marks a limit to their abilities. These learners may set themselves appropriate Learning Challenges, targeting a level of difficulty slightly beyond their current best. But if these learners only focus on *what* they are learning and not *how* they are learning, they will not succeed in the Learning Challenge and will remain stuck at the bottom of the pit.

In schools, we see this all the time. There is too much focus on *what* learners are learning, and not enough on *how* learners are learning. There is too much attention given to the ground (curriculum) being covered, and typically too little to how learners move through this.

THE LEARNING LANDSCAPE

This doesn't pose a significant problem when the curriculum only demands from learners more "easy things they haven't done yet". In this case, learners can get by, sometimes for years, with what they currently have in their backpack. But as the standards and, therefore, the level of difficulty and complexity in the curriculum increase, learners find they are no longer equipped to succeed.

Both the teacher and the student need to appreciate that succeeding in increasingly difficult tasks requires the development of increasingly mature Habits of Mind. If the focus is purely on what the student is learning and not on increasing Learner Agency to become a better learner, then teachers may be setting learners up to fail.

DEVELOPING THE HABITS OF MIND

To become a skilful learner, students must develop their Habits of Mind and learn how to more skilfully and mindfully engage in them. There are five ways to get better at the Habits, which we refer to as the Dimensions of Growth[23].

❶ MEANING: WHAT

Although we may feel we understand what each Habit of Mind means, behind each is great depth and richness of meaning. As we grow and develop each Habit of Mind, we delve into it, understanding it more deeply. As teachers, we are then able to draw on richer examples and provide more insightful definitions for learners.

For example, a young learner might define the Habit of Mind of "Persistence" as simply "not giving up", citing the example of "the little engine that could". This level of understanding might be sufficient for, say, a 5-year-old.

As the learner becomes more sophisticated, they may come to understand that this is a shallow definition. Persistence includes finding other ways to reach a goal. Furthermore, knowing when to quit is equally as important as knowing when to keep going.

Obviously, there are more insightful examples of persistence than "the little engine that could". For example, we could draw on examples of people who persisted in the face of unexpected adversity or when the distance to their goal was unknown and unknowable.

CHAPTER 4: HABITS OF MIND

Each step towards a deeper understanding of a Habit of Mind helps learners develop that Habit and fills a student's backpack a little more.

❷ CAPACITY: HOW

Each Habit of Mind involves a set of actions that define how learners engage in it. These are skills or tools that may be cognitive (e.g. thought process) or concrete (e.g. a graphic organiser).

For example, for many people, the Habit of Mind of "Creating, Imagining and Innovating" only involves an effort to "dream up new ideas". In this case, there would be few strategies or tools in the learner's backpack, which may be sufficient in the lowlands where tasks aren't particularly challenging but may be insufficient on higher ground.

Edward de Bono is a champion of deliberate creative thinking tools. He points out that creativity, far from being a free-roaming, brainstorming type of thinking, can be highly deliberate and skilful.[24] As a highly skilled creative thinker, he has created tools such as "escaping the dominant idea", "Random Inputs", "5 Whys" and many others. Becoming fluent in the application of these creative thinking tools develops the Habit of Mind of Creating, Imagining and Innovating, and fills your backpack.

As learners build their repertoire of skills and tools for each Habit of Mind, they fill their backpacks, become more proficient at engaging in the Habit, build Learner Agency and are thus better able to take on increasingly difficult challenges.

❸ ALERTNESS: WHEN

Knowing which Habits of Mind to use is of critical importance. Learners must become sensitive to recognising which circumstances call for which Habits of Mind. Developing a Habit of Mind involves becoming more alert to the subtle cues and signals in the environment that alert the learner to when, and when not, to engage in a Habit of Mind.

THE LEARNING LANDSCAPE

For example, we don't want learners to use all the Habits all the time. Someone who "Strives for Accuracy" all the time would be called a perfectionist. It's important to recognise those occasions when "near enough" really is good enough and the learner's time is better spent moving on. Someone who "Thinks Flexibly" all the time could be considered wishy-washy and indecisive. As important as this Habit is, it is equally as important to recognise when to stop thinking flexibly to deepen and consolidate the ideas generated.

For learners to get better at the Habits of Mind and fill their backpacks, they must learn to recognise the signals that tell them when they should engage each Habit. Early in development, these signals may be as overt as direct feedback from the teacher to check their work ("Strive for Accuracy"). Later, they may be as subtle as recognising a slight change in a person's tone or inflection that indicates they are making an important point and it is thus a time to bring to bear your skills in Listen with Empathy and Understanding.

❹ VALUE: WHY

Development of a learner's Habits of Mind also occurs as they learn to recognise the value and benefits that arise from engaging in them.

For example, initially, the only value a learner may see in "Managing Impulsivity" is that they get into less trouble or receive a gold star. Here, the value is extrinsic and relatively trivial.

Over time, as they develop their appreciation of how the Habits of Mind help them grow and reach their goals, they begin to value them more intrinsically. They recognise the broad benefits the Habits of Mind bring to their learning in general, seeing them as versatile tools that help them approach many different challenges.

❺ COMMITMENT: HOW WELL

A learner's ability to self-assess and self-direct their development of the Habits of Mind is the final Dimension of Growth.

In the lowlands, when the application of the Habits of Mind need not be very sophisticated, it may be enough for learners to simply identify when they did or didn't use a Habit of Mind. They might then progress to a general sense of knowing whether they used them poorly or used them well.

CHAPTER 4: HABITS OF MIND

As they continue to develop their capacity to self-assess and self-direct, they become increasingly qualitative and descriptive in terms of assessing how well they engage in the Habits of Mind. As teachers, we need to identify areas of improvement and strategies to help them achieve that development. And they will need to become increasingly accurate in their self-evaluation of their ability to skilfully and mindfully engage in each Habit of Mind.

This does not necessarily mean the learner engages in the Habits of Mind well. It simply means they are perceptive and accurate in their self-evaluation, as well as in their ability to plan their own development.

These five Dimensions of Growth define what it means to get better at the Habits of Mind. They explain how learners can fill their backpacks with increasingly well-developed Habits of Mind so they are prepared to take on increasingly difficult tasks and become more efficacious learners.

THE BENEFITS OF BECOMING A BETTER CLIMBER

How well developed a learner's Habits of Mind are, and how well they've filled their backpack, defines how high they can climb in the Learning Landscape.

The better equipped the learner is, the more difficult the tasks they can succeed at and the higher they can climb. This is why we only find the best-equipped learners on the highest peaks.

But we don't find the best-equipped climbers *only* on the highest peaks. We see them throughout the Learning Landscape. Unlike less well-equipped learners restricted to the lowlands, well-equipped learners are free to roam far and wide, high and low, throughout the Learning Landscape.

The real benefit of filling learners' backpacks is that it gives them the freedom to choose where they want to go in the Learning Landscape. It allows them to raise the bar and increase their Comfort Zone, so more and more tasks become "easy things they haven't done yet".

THE LEARNING LANDSCAPE

As the story of Turia Pitt shows (see the end of this chapter), having reached the highest peaks in one domain equips learners with the skills necessary to excel more quickly in new domains. A learner's backpack goes with them wherever they travel in the Learning Landscape. Although someone may be an expert with a lot of "ground beneath their feet" in one area, as they move to a new domain, they still must acquire the new knowledge and understandings of that domain. Being an expert in one field does not make someone an instant expert in another; they still must the travel the Learning Landscape, but because they have their well-equipped backpack with them, the journey is much easier!

One of the few certainties in life is that it is unpredictable. Inevitably, learners will confront challenges or adversities that exceed their current abilities. Even if their backpacks are sufficient for most of what they do in their day-to-day lives, at the very least, learners must know they are capable of filling their backpacks further when they need to confront those challenges. Better still, they can prepare for an uncertain future by filling their backpacks before the challenges and adversities arise. If they are not in the habit of filling their backpacks, then learners will inevitably be confronted with challenges that will be forever beyond their reach.

Agile Learners understand this better than anyone. As we'll see below, different learners have different attitudes towards filling their backpacks. For the Agile Learner, challenges are primarily there to help them fill their backpacks, so they build the capacity to take on whatever challenges they choose or that circumstance demands of them. They understand that the better learner they become, the more agile, responsive and successful they'll be at meeting the demands of an unpredictable world.

HOW DIFFERENT LEARNERS RELATE TO THEIR BACKPACK

Different types of learners take different approaches to filling their backpacks with well-developed Habits of Mind.

The descriptions below are intended to help you identify the different types of learners in your classroom. It's important to remember that this does not classify them in any permanent way; instead, it helps you pinpoint where learners are at the moment, then identify ways to help move them towards being more Agile Learners.

CHAPTER 4: HABITS OF MIND

NON-LEARNERS

Non-Learners are **ignorant** of their learning behaviours. Because they so rarely engage in any significant learning, they lack even a basic vocabulary to describe their learning behaviours. They don't know what's in their backpack and they don't truly engage in learning. For them, they do what they can do, and don't do what they can't. That's it.

BEGINNING LEARNERS

Beginning Learners can **describe** their learning behaviours, but usually retrospectively. They know what's in their backpack, even if it's not very much.

These learners are at least moving around the Learning Landscape, even if they seek to minimise challenges and move downhill most of the time. They can describe what they did while they were learning and tell you which Habits of Mind they took out of their backpack for a given task.

There is little deliberateness in the way Beginning Learners apply their Habits of Mind, and certainly no intent to get better at them. Their backpacks are usually small.

PERFORMANCE LEARNERS

Performance Learners **apply** their full complement of Habits of Mind to the task at hand. They want to perform their best, so they use what they have to succeed. They are, of course, careful not to choose a task that outstrips their current abilities, which could lead to failure.

These learners are much more familiar with what's in their backpack and can describe the sort of learning behaviours required for a given task. They are predictive as well as reflective.

At other times, Performance Learners may have been Above-the-Line learners (either Directed or Independent Learners), so it's possible their backpacks are quite full. But unless they set themselves new goals or find themselves in a structured environment that will help them fill their backpacks, they are no longer actively developing their Habits of Mind. Their performance has plateaued. Their standard may be high (or not), but whatever it is, it is stable. They are not getting better.

THE LEARNING LANDSCAPE

DIRECTED LEARNERS

Directed Learners seek to **extend** their Habits of Mind so they can meet the demands of a Learning Challenge.

These learners understand that to raise the standard they are at, to climb higher in the Learning Landscape, they cannot rely on what's currently in their backpack. They recognise the need to become better climbers.

These learners need significant direction, scaffolding and support to develop their Habits of Mind and add to their backpacks. They mainly rely on the teacher to fill their backpacks for them, trusting them to equip them for the Learning Challenge.

INDEPENDENT LEARNERS

Independent Learners actively **develop** their Habits of Mind. They understand that to raise their standards, they need to become better learners.

Compared to the Directed Learner, Independent Learners are much more self-directed in the development of their Habits of Mind. They target specific learning behaviours they have identified as necessary to reach particular goals.

The Independent Learner's primary focus is on reaching their goal. They understand that to do this they will need to also focus on how they are learning. Filling their backpack is merely a necessary step towards reaching their goal.

For example, a student who is an Independent Learner may have set themselves the goal of reaching a certain standard in their study of science. This student would look carefully at the Far Side of the Challenge Pit, recognise it as a Learning Challenge and identify the standards and success criteria. Recognising that they are not currently capable of producing the standard of performance required, they might identify that the disposition they need to develop is "Questioning and Posing Problems" – specifically, developing a testable hypothesis. They would then seek ways to develop this Habit of Mind so they can reach the goal they've set for themselves. Note that this learner's primary driver is reaching the standard.

For the Independent Learner, the goal comes first; then they work on developing their Habits of Mind to match the need. This development takes time and may result in lost opportunities if the environment is changing rapidly. Agile Learners, on the other hand, invest in filling their backpacks before the need arises.

CHAPTER 4: HABITS OF MIND

AGILE LEARNERS

Agile Learners actively **cultivate** their Habits of Mind. They are highly aware of themselves as learners and see the development of their Habits of Mind as the primary goal of learning.

Agile Learners treasure their backpacks. They are all about filling their backpacks and becoming better climbers. They understand that being a well-equipped climber will help them overcome whatever challenge or adversity they face. They seek and embrace challenges, avoiding easy tasks specifically to develop their Habits of Mind.

Agile Learners are primarily focused on becoming better learners. To them, climbing out of the pit and succeeding at a Learning Challenge is simply evidence they have become better learners.

The Agile Learner's focus on filling their backpack makes them extremely adaptable and flexible. As opportunities arise, or they are forced to face adversity, they are often better equipped to take advantage of them than Independent or Directed Learners.

OPPORTUNITIES

Educators talk a lot about giving students opportunities. But what do we really mean? How do we give students true opportunities in life?

When people talk about opportunities, often what they really mean is circumstances. You're said to have an opportunity if you are in the right place, at the right time, with the right resources around you. But in reality, this is only one aspect of an opportunity.

True opportunities only exist when the correct circumstances exist in concert with the desire and ability to take advantage of those circumstances. Without the right circumstances, the opportunity is lost and the learner will become frustrated. But opportunity is also lost whenever the learner lacks the desire and/or ability to take advantage of the opportunity.

A learner might be in the right place at the right time but lack the desire to take advantage of these circumstances. They are simply disinterested.

Lack of desire isn't always a problem. Schools often present learners with many options, providing all the circumstances to make this possible, but learners are not expected to follow them all.

THE LEARNING LANDSCAPE

Educators should be concerned if disinterest is due to a Fixed Mindset (see *Chapter 6: Mindset*). These learners incorrectly believe they are limited to just one part of the Learning Landscape. Consequently, when circumstances arise that might allow them to explore another part of the Learning Landscape, they are disinterested and fail to take advantage of them. They believe they are limited because of the "type of person" they are.

For example, a learner who believes they are musical (and only musical) will stick solely to the part of the Learning Landscape the contains music. They act as if other parts of it are "off limits" to them. When circumstances arise that might let them explore and even excel in another part of the Learning Landscape, they lack motivation. They incorrectly believe the opportunity is not truly available to them.

This highlights what we've said before. There's a big difference between not getting better at something because you don't want to, and not getting better at something because you don't believe you can.

Circumstance and interest are just two elements of an opportunity. An opportunity doesn't exist unless a learner is empowered to take advantage of it. And this is where filling a backpack with the Habits of Mind comes in.

Without the ability to act on their interest and the circumstances around them, a learner is impotent in the face of the opportunity. On the other hand, learners who spend their time filling their backpacks and increasing their Learner Agency position themselves for future success. When circumstance and interest align, they are prepared to take advantage of the opportunity. Instead of being impotent in the face of opportunity, they are empowered.

The Agile Learner is particularly aware of how filling their backpack empowers them to take advantage of circumstances when they arise. Their primary concern is to use opportunities to cultivate their Habits of Mind.

These learners are motivated, in part, by circumstances that allow them to develop their Habits of Mind and fill their backpacks, knowing that this helps better prepare them to succeed in future opportunities and to face adversity.

The Agile Learner also understands that life isn't always about opportunities. Opportunity implies choice. But sometimes learners don't really get to choose. In the context of an uncertain, volatile, changeable and ambiguous world, circumstances may arise that give the learner no choice but to act. These adversities are more likely to be overcome if the learner is well prepared and already has a backpack full of well-developed Habits of Mind.

CHAPTER 4: HABITS OF MIND

Of the three elements of an opportunity, the one that is most within the learner's control is ability. It is also the one that can take the longest to develop. Circumstance can come and go in a moment. Adversity can replace desire with necessity. The learner who empowers themselves by developing their Habits of Mind will ultimately be best prepared to benefit from opportunities.

TEACHER ACTION: FILLING THE BACKPACK

Introduce the Habits of Mind to your class as a common way of describing learning behaviours (there are some great resources at **www.habitsofmind.org** to help you do this).

Use the language of the Habits of Mind to describe how learners in your classroom need to behave to get out of a Challenge Pit, especially Learning Challenges.

Ask learners to draw or describe their "backpacks", detailing what learning behaviours they already have in their backpacks. Where are their current strengths and areas of improvement?

As you begin a learning activity, ask students to identify the Habits of Mind that are likely to be most important and will help them get out of the pit.

When students are struggling in the bottom of a Challenge Pit, help them identify which Habits of Mind they need to draw on or develop to climb out.

Help students understand that each time they call upon a Habit of Mind, they won't necessarily use it the same way. They should learn to be more efficacious and mature in their application of the Habits of Mind. They are tools in development.

Use examples like Turia Pitt to highlight that no matter which part of the Learning Landscape learners might be exploring today, filling their backpack will always help them succeed at other Learning Challenges in other parts of the Learning Landscape. Discuss how filling their backpack lets learners "turn their hand" to many other challenges.

Emphasise that everyone can fill their backpack and become a better climber. Climbing skills are not a part of who a learner is; they are a part of how they learn to climb.

THE LEARNING LANDSCAPE

TURIA PITT

Turia Pitt knows how to take on challenges and overcome adversity.

Completing a double degree combining a Bachelor of Engineering (Mining) and Bachelor of Science at the University of New South Wales in 2010, Pitt went on to successfully apply her learning as a mining engineer at a prestigious diamond mining company in Western Australia.

Not content with only pursuing academic and career goals, Pitt also excelled in many other areas. She was a contestant in the Miss Earth Australia beauty pageant and a professional model. She was also a successful ultramarathon runner.

Having reached significant milestones in her various pursuits, Pitt had proven her capacity for setting and achieving difficult goals. In the context of the Learning Landscape, she had filled her backpack with well-developed Habits of Mind and applied these to succeed at her chosen pursuits. She was roaming high in the Learning Landscape, taking on Learning Challenges, succeeding and heading higher!

Tragically, on 2 September 2011, while competing in a 100-kilometre ultramarathon in the Kimberly region of Western Australia, Pitt was caught in a grassfire and suffered burns to 65 per cent of her body, including her face. She was placed in a medically induced coma for six months, underwent more than 200 operations, had her left foot amputated, and lost all the fingers on her left hand and two on her right. In total, she spent more than two years in hospital recovering from her burns.

Obviously, Pitt's life would never be the same. To say she'd suffered a setback would be an understatement. But she did not let the events of September 2011 define her. She understood that although circumstances beyond her control had radically changed her life, she was still able to grow. She knew how to overcome challenges and her backpack was still full of the Habits of Mind she had developed prior to her accident. She had to use those same skills to overcome the adversity she now faced.

In the years that followed her recovery from the accident, Pitt took on many new challenges. These included:

- completing a Master of Business Administration from Southern Cross University
- competing in Ironman events, including the gruelling Hawaii Ironman
- trekking the Great Wall of China and the Kokoda Trail
- authoring bestselling books, including Everything to Live For and Unmasked

CHAPTER 4: HABITS OF MIND

- becoming a sought-after and acclaimed speaker, headlining the National Achievers Congress in Brisbane in 2018
- being named as a finalist for Young Australian of the Year and Australian of the Year
- qualifying as the New South Wales' finalist for the Telstra Business Women's Awards
- being named as one of the Westpac Women of Influence 2015
- founding the School of Champions to show others how to achieve their goals.

How has she been able to achieve so much? Pitt credits much of her success to her mindset (see **Chapter 6: Mindset**). She understands that the person she is today does not have to be the person she is tomorrow. She knows she's capable of moving freely through the Learning Landscape.

But understanding you're capable of growth is not the same as achieving it. It takes more than believing in yourself to climb to the highest heights and move freely through the Learning Landscape. You don't believe your way to the kind of success Pitt has achieved – you must act your way there.

On her School of Champions website, Pitt says: "Don't fall into the trap of thinking I've been able to do all of that because I'm 'just like that' ... It's just that I've picked up some really bloody powerful, and totally learnable, strategies along the way."[25]

Yes, Pitt believes in herself, but she backs that up with action. She has filled, and continues to fill, her backpack with well-developed Habits of Mind. Although she might use different names for her actions, these are the dispositions that allow her to succeed at increasingly difficult challenges. She carries these Habits of Mind with her as she travels widely in the Learning Landscape, taking on challenges as diverse as Ironman competitions, writing, public speaking, master's degrees and starting her own "School of Champions".

Pitt's mindset is what encourages her to jump into these very different Challenge Pits. But it is her Habits of Mind that allow her to climb out and succeed at those increasingly difficult challenges. In short, she knows what it takes to climb out of a Challenge Pit – any Challenge Pit!

The great advantage of climbing high in the Learning Landscape is that you must fill your backpack with well-developed Habits of Mind. Once in your backpack, these can be applied to all your travels in the Learning Landscape. Simply having a full backpack does not make you an expert in other parts of the Learning Landscape, but it does ensure you're well equipped for the journey to these new lands!

PROFESSOR ANDERS ERICSSON: PRACTICE

Conradi Eminent Scholar and Professor of Psychology at Florida State University, Anders Ericsson is referred to as the "Expertise Expert". A large part of his academic career has focused on studies of the acquisition of expert performance. His research spans areas as diverse as the acquisition of talents in medicine, music, chess, memory and flying military fighter jets! His observations about how learners develop their abilities to become elite performers have profound implications for educators.

His publications include *Toward a General Theory of Expertise* (with Jacqui Smith, 1991) and *The Road to Excellence: The Acquisition of Expert Performance in the Arts and Sciences, Sports and* Games (1996). He is also the co-editor of *The Cambridge Handbook of Expertise and Expert Performance* (2006). His most recent publication, *Peak: Secrets from the New Science of Expertise* (2016) was co-authored with Robert Pool and written for a non-academic audience.

Of all the great thinkers mentioned in this book, Ericsson's work is perhaps the least well-known by school-based educators. It is my sincere hope that this book brings this important work to the attention of more educators. His insights into talent acquisition are critical to the learning process and need to be better understood and applied in the classroom context.

Ericsson helps us understand the process of moving through the Learning Landscape and what is required to climb the mountains of expertise. He highlights the importance of distinguishing Downhill and Performance Challenges from Learning Challenges. Ericsson also helps us understand why there are no limits to a learner's growth and extends our understanding of human potential when he points out that "learning isn't a way of reaching one's potential; rather, it is a way of developing it."[26]

Perhaps most importantly, Ericsson's work dispels the myth of natural talent and provides a researched-based explanation as to how learners acquire talents through practice.

CHAPTER 5
PRACTICE

It takes more than filling a backpack for learners to climb out of a Challenge Pit and succeed at Learning Challenges. Filling their backpack is the preparation. To succeed in a Learning Challenge, learners must act, and that means *climbing* out of the pit.

Climbing out is the act of applying the Habits of Mind to the challenge. This process is rarely straightforward. A learner may be well-equipped for the climb, but that does not mean the climb will be without its challenges!

Climbing out takes time and effort. A struggle is often involved. Mistakes are made and must be responded to. Learners also gather feedback during the climb to improve their efforts and succeed in the challenge.

In this chapter, we will look at the process of climbing out of a Challenge Pit and the role mistakes and feedback have in this process. We will draw on and apply the work of Anders Ericsson, the expertise expert, to the Learning Landscape.

Ericsson describes the "3 Fs of Practice".[27] These are:
1. Focus: the learner focuses on what they are trying to achieve.
2. Feedback: the learner gathers meaningful feedback on their progress.
3. Fix It: the learner fixes mistakes to reach the new standard.

Additionally, between the **Focus** on where a learner is going and the **Feedback** on how they're going is what we recognise as the struggle of the climb.

THE LEARNING LANDSCAPE

VIRTUOUS PRACTICE[28]

One of the central tenants of Ericsson's work is that if you never push yourself beyond your current best, you will never improve. In the context of the Learning Landscape, this concept becomes especially clear. In order to get better, you have to attempt to climb higher in the Learning Landscape. Reaching the highest peaks in the Learning Landscape identifies you as an expert in that area.

But one of the things we notice about the Learning Landscape is that some of the peaks of expertise have clear paths marking the best and quickest route to the summit. These paths are often travelled by groups of students, who are guided by some of the experts who have previously climbed to the summit.

These well-worn paths are to be found in areas where people have been exploring the Learning Landscape for many, many years. These are areas like classical music, mathematics, many martial arts and other similarly mature fields where there is broad agreement on what expertise looks like, as well as the best path(s) to follow in order to reach it.

It is in these parts of the Learning Landscape that learners can gain height most quickly. While each learner must still undertake their own journey, their journey is informed by the many others who have gone before.

Ericsson describes this type of practice that follows a well-worn path as Deliberate Practice. It is what he refers to as the "Gold Standard" of practice.[29] Previous climbers have marked out the best and shortest paths and are there to guide the way.

But not all of the higher ground in the Learning Landscape is as well signposted. This happens whenever a learner is exploring parts of the Learning Landscape that hasn't been explored before. This might include the expert who is seeking even higher peaks. It would also include areas where there is no agreed-on peak that defines expertise, such as parenting. In these situations, each learner has to find their own way.

Ericsson describes this sort of practice as being Purposeful Practice.[30] With no clear path for the learner to follow they have to make their own way higher in the Learning Landscape.

Both Purposeful and Deliberate Practice have several common elements. Firstly, they both involve Learning Challenges – challenges that result in the learner climbing higher in the learning landscape. Secondly, they both engage the learner in the 3 Fs of climbing explained below.

CHAPTER 5: PRACTICE

For the sake of clarity, I have chosen to use the term Virtuous Practice to include both Purposeful and Deliberate Practice. The virtue of this sort of practice is that it results in the learner gaining height and expertise in the Learning Landscape.

CLIMBING

Ericsson tells us there are three critical elements to getting better: Focus, Feedback and Fix It.

❶ FOCUS

Focus is about setting clear Learning Challenges that are just beyond the learner's current best. It's about knowing what success will look like. In short, it's the ability to identify the Far Side of the Challenge Pit. Focus is about knowing where you're heading in the Learning Landscape.

Ericsson points out that improvement isn't a general occurrence. It's highly specific.[31] It's about the learner understanding specifically what their learning goals and objectives are, and how they'll know when they've achieved them. Importantly, these learning goals must be slightly beyond the learner's current best. Improvement does not happen when they do *more* work. Improvement occurs when they attempt *harder* work.

For example, the student who spends all day perfectly completing work they have done before will not experience growth. The student who spends an hour identifying and focusing on the part of the work they can't currently do by responding to mistakes, seeking help and correcting those mistakes is more likely to achieve real growth.

Improvement is much more than a general desire to get better or a long-term goal. Improvement relies on setting (many) small, incremental goals – each clearly defined and each slightly more demanding than the last. These are the Learning Challenges described in the previous chapter.

In the context of the Learning Landscape, Focus is the difference between the learner being able to identify the Far Side of the Challenge Pit and "heading in the general direction of that mountain over there". The former leads to improvement. The latter is likely to lead to frustration.

Having clear learning goals that represent small increases in difficulty and having explicit success criteria that tell learners when they have reached these goals is the perfect way to achieve Focus. Curriculum and assessment practices set these goals

THE LEARNING LANDSCAPE

and criteria in our schools. But in real life, we often forget the importance of Focus. We set ourselves vague goals like "becoming a better parent" or "getting a promotion at work". These sorts of goals fall into the "heading in that general direction" category.

Focus is about knowing exactly what the Far Side of the Challenge Pit looks like. It also involves knowing or finding out what needs to be in the learner's backpack to get there.

PRODUCTIVE AND UNPRODUCTIVE STRUGGLE

All movement through the Learning Landscape involves expending time and energy – what we often refer to as "effort". Moving downhill is easier than moving uphill, so the type of effort involved will be different depending on whether the challenge is uphill or downhill. Nonetheless, both require the expenditure of time and energy, even though the result of spending that time and energy will be different – an idea we will explore more deeply in *Chapter 7: Effort*.

Sometimes when learners engage in a Learning Challenge, attempting something more difficult than they've done before, they can feel as though they are getting nowhere. Despite the fact the right level of challenge has been set, and they have prepared themselves by filling their backpacks, progress can slow or even stop. Every learner experiences this; it's a normal part of the learning process. The time and energy learners spend trying to get out of the pit increases, and progress stops. In this situation, learners may begin to feel frustrated that they are receiving little or no reward for their effort. They feel as though they are clambering up the Far Side of the Challenge Pit, only to slide back down again. This is called "Unproductive Struggle".

As we'll explore in *Chapter 6: Mindset*, if learners remain in Unproductive Struggle, seeing little or no gain for their effort, they may eventually come to the belief that their efforts are wasted and give up permanently.

To succeed and climb out of a Challenge Pit, we need to help learners turn Unproductive Struggle into Productive Struggle. Productive Struggle acknowledges that changing the standard a learner is working at requires the expenditure of time and energy. There will be times when progress slows or even stops temporarily. But it's vital that learners use the struggle to inform and guide their learning and, ultimately, see progress resume.

The difference between Unproductive and Productive Struggle is information, and this information comes in the form of feedback. The most effective learners are adept at recognising Unproductive Struggle and take measures to turn it into Productive Struggle by seeking out sources of new information.

As we've discussed, there is nothing about any individual learner that prevents them from reaching the highest peaks of the Learning Landscape. Success is not about

CHAPTER 5: PRACTICE

who they are; it's about what they do. So, when a learner finds themselves stuck in a Challenge Pit, in Unproductive Struggle, it is not because of some permanent limit to their abilities; rather, it is a lack of understanding about how to extend their abilities and climb out of the pit.

To move from Unproductive Struggle to Productive Struggle, the learner needs *information* about why they are stuck and what to do about it. The role of feedback is to provide this information.

❷ FEEDBACK

Feedback provides the information learners need to fine-tune their progress. It helps them overcome Unproductive Struggle and turn it into Productive Struggle so they can resume progress towards their goals and climb out of a Challenge Pit.

There are two broad sources of feedback. Firstly, there is the feedback provided by the learners' efforts. Every mistake, every misstep, every failed attempt, every time the learner recognises they are not where they intended to be, offers information that can inform their journey through the Learning Landscape. At a minimum, a mistake tells learners, "Don't do that." A well-designed mistake provides much more detailed, insightful and helpful information.

Secondly, there is feedback that is external to the learner. It often comes from a teacher or expert who has previously explored that part of the Learning Landscape. These people can provide information the learner may not have been able to discern themselves.

Tomes have been written about the best timing and format of feedback. In the context of the Learning Landscape it is important to recognise that feedback is, in its broadest context, information that guides the learning journey.

Feedback acts as a signpost in the Learning Landscape. It points learners in the right direction and highlights the tools they need to put in their backpacks. But feedback can only do this if learners can read the signs and if they listen to the feedback.

MISTAKES AND OTHER SIGNPOSTS

Mistakes are the slips and falls, the missteps and stumbles, learners make as they try to climb out of a Challenge Pit, especially when taking on Learning Challenges. They are not signs of failure. They are a natural part of the learning process; the product of the struggle necessary to climb out of a pit. In the first instance, mistakes provide

THE LEARNING LANDSCAPE

information that highlights the gap between where a learner is and where they want to be. When a learner makes a mistake, it tells them they have not reached their goal of climbing out of a Challenge Pit.

We don't need to think of mistakes as the traditional "got it wrong". Mistakes are simply gaps in knowledge that should direct learners towards where they want to be. There are also other types of "gaps" learners can use as signposts. Something all of these have in common is that they create cognitive dissonance in the learner that provides potentially rich sources of information. These include:

- **a problem.** When learners confront a problem they don't immediately know the answer to, this problem highlights a gap between where they are and where they want to be. A problem is a bit like recognising a mistake before it's made. In the context of the Learning Landscape, recognising a problem is like asking, "How do I get over there?"

- **inconsistencies or incongruences.** Sometimes things don't add up. One set of data suggests one answer, while a second suggests another. These inconsistencies or incongruences highlight that learners are not yet where they want to be. At times, these gaps can be highly informative

- **falling short or missing the mark.** Sometimes learners set a target and don't quite reach it. That doesn't necessarily mean they've got something wrong. It simply highlights that perhaps the learner didn't get it as "right" as they would have liked

- **continuous improvement.** Where a learner is in the Learning Landscape might be perfectly okay, but there's often an opportunity to do better. The gap between good and better offers learners the same sort of learning opportunity as falling short – it's just another gap between where they are and where they want to be

- **alternatives.** Searching for a different way to do something can point the way towards future growth. It's like asking, "Is there another path to where I want to go?" The act of finding that new path can uncover new understandings

- **experts.** Someone who has explored that part of the Learning Landscape before can point out places the learner didn't even know they needed to go. The expert can point to gaps the learner might not have recognised for themselves.

It's important to recognise that all the above, from mistakes to experts, serve the same basic purpose. They highlight a gap between where the learner is and where they want to be. They are a way of informing the learner's journey through the Learning Landscape. They point them in the direction they need to go.

CHAPTER 5: PRACTICE

This is important because traditionally, some learners have looked at mistakes as negative things to avoid. More recently, the reverse approach has been adopted and mistakes have been celebrated as proof that learners are engaged in learning. But while mistakes might be proof a learner is trying, they are also proof they are not growing, and ultimately it is the growth that is important, not just the attempt to grow.

In the context of the Learning Landscape, mistakes are simply a source of information. Mistakes are neither good nor bad. They are merely signposts that point learners in the direction of their future learning.

No matter how we define mistakes, and despite them being part of the learning process, they still aren't signs of success. Catchphrases such as "mistakes are proof you are trying" mislead us into thinking the important part is that the learner is trying. This is not the case.

Mistakes are proof that learners are engaged in the learning process, which is good, but they are also proof that they have not yet succeeded. The critical aspect of a mistake is that the learner extracts information from it to turn Unproductive Struggle into Productive Struggle so they can eventually succeed. Until the learner corrects the mistake, what Ericsson would call the "Fix It" part of the process, they have not reached their goal of climbing out of the pit.

HELPFUL AND UNHELPFUL MISTAKES

It's useful to distinguish between two broad categories of mistakes: helpful and unhelpful mistakes. The difference between these sorts of mistakes comes down to the amount of information they provide.

Unhelpful mistakes provide little or no new information to help progress a student's learning. They may be signposts, but what those signposts say is either so obvious the learner doesn't need it pointed out, or so obscure that the student doesn't know what the signposts are telling them.

Helpful mistakes provide information that acts as a signpost in the Learning Landscape. The more useful information a mistake offers, the more helpful it is.

To illustrate this point, consider a common meme associated with mistakes. Attributed to inventor Thomas Edison is the phrase, "I have not failed. I've just found 10 000 ways that won't work." If each of these 10 000 failures only provided the information that "this does not work", it could be said to be, at best, minimally helpful and unhelpful

THE LEARNING LANDSCAPE

mistakes at worst. Was Edison going to go on trying every possible way of making a light globe until he stumbled onto the one way that worked?

Encouraging learners to make these sorts of mistakes does little to help them climb out of a Challenge Pit. It would be the equivalent of asking them to mindlessly throw themselves at the Far Side of a Challenge Pit and hope they find a way out.

This highlights the problem with the generalised "praise mistakes" approach frequently adopted in schools today. It's not the mistake that's important, but the *information* the learner can take from that mistake, and how they then act on it.

But Edison was not trying different ways to find a design and filament that would make an electric light work at random. He was a scientist, and each test he conducted was designed in a specific way so it would provide maximum information to get him closer to a light globe that worked. He controlled variables, asked meaningful questions and carefully collected data that told him much more than "this doesn't work". He used the information gained from his mistakes to rule out whole categories of approaches and to point him in the most promising direction. His mistakes were information rich, not random errors.

Instead of praising learners for their mistakes, we should praise them for taking on Learning Challenges. Praise them for recognising what their mistakes tell them and the actions they take as a result. Praise them for their growth. But don't praise – or make them feel bad for making – their mistakes. Mistakes are not good or bad; they are signposts that point learners in the direction of future learning. Praise learners for reading and responding to these signposts.

MISTAKES IN DIFFERENT ZONES

It is also useful to consider the types of mistakes likely to occur in different zones.[32]

Learners are unlikely to make many helpful mistakes in their Comfort Zone. Mistakes made here are often the result of carelessness. When they occur, they remind learners of something they already knew, rather than providing new information that might help them grow. For example, when an adult makes a careless arithmetic error when totalling a bill, the lesson is to pay attention to what they are doing – something they already knew – rather than learn how to be better at addition.

When learners are in their Performance Zone, they try to avoid mistakes. There are many instances when errors are undesirable, and not all occasions are desirable

CHAPTER 5: PRACTICE

learning opportunities. We don't want to make mistakes when the stakes are high or when we need to do our best – for example, during a test, while landing aircraft or performing heart surgery. In these situations, we can learn from any mistakes made, but by virtue of the fact we are trying to minimise the chance of errors occurring, they are not good learning opportunities.

Sloppy mistakes and high-stakes mistakes occur below the line. As such, they hold limited opportunity to inform growth.

The types of mistakes we want learners to make are called stretch mistakes. These mistakes occur above the line, in the Learning Zone. These are the mistakes learners must become comfortable with and recognise for their learning potential.

Stretch mistakes are mistakes learners make intentionally. This is not to say they deliberately make these mistakes; rather, they go into their Learning Zone knowing the task is beyond their current ability, then look for what their mistakes tell them about how to develop those abilities.

EXTERNAL FEEDBACK

Information about a learner's progress that comes from an outside source is generally described as feedback. This external feedback can come from a person, such as a teacher or expert. It can also come from machines or other measuring devices. In either case, this sort of feedback follows the same basic rules as we've discussed. To be useful, feedback must contain specific information about the learner's progress through the pit. This information must be discernible and understood by the learner, then acted upon.

❸ FIX IT

It is not enough for learners to only know what it is they are trying to achieve and to receive feedback about their progress towards that goal. Ultimately, they need to respond to the feedback given, modify their actions and achieve their goal.

Too often, learners leave their learning journey incomplete when they:
- focus on what it is they are trying to achieve
- receive feedback on why they have not reached their goal
- move on to the next challenge without having completed the first!

"Moving on" without first mastering a task is a bit like acknowledging that you can see the path out of the Challenge Pit, but not bothering to climb out!

In the context of the Learning Landscape, a learner has not succeeded in their learning journey until they reach the other side of the pit. In order to gain the new knowledge and understanding they must complete the climb out of the pit.

Providing feedback about what to do next, without both equipping the student to climb out and allowing them the opportunity to engage in the climb, is to rob them of true learning.

To help learners to get out of the pit, the teacher – having identified which Habits of Mind the learner needs to develop – needs to help the student fill their backpack, thereby equipping them for the climb. The learner must then complete the climb in order to gain the new knowledge and understandings.

HOW DIFFERENT LEARNERS RELATE TO MISTAKES AND FEEDBACK

As you might imagine, different learners create and use mistakes and feedback differently.

NON-LEARNERS

Non-Learners **ignore** their mistakes and **disregard** feedback.

To make a mistake, the learner first needs to act. In many instances, Non-Learners do so little travelling through the Learning Landscape that there is little opportunity for mistakes. Any mistakes they do make are likely to be ignored.

Non-Learners disregard external feedback. Feedback for this type of learner is often about what they should be doing rather than correcting what they have done, so they usually ignore it as they are disinclined to move through the Learning Landscape.

BEGINNING LEARNERS

Beginning Learners **recognise** mistakes and **acknowledge** feedback.

Unlike Non-Learners, Beginning Learners at least move through the Learning Landscape. But because they are well within their Comfort Zone and minimise challenges most of

CHAPTER 5: PRACTICE

the time, any mistakes they do make are likely to be sloppy mistakes. These are often caused by carelessness rather than stretching themselves beyond their current ability, so they hold little, if any, useful information about how to improve.

One of the key characteristics of the Beginning Learner is that they don't see themselves as improvers. They don't go uphill, and they don't fill their backpacks. As a result, for this type of learner, what's done is done. Something that is done incorrectly is just the way they do it – they recognise they may not have got it right, but they see little they can do about it.

Feedback is received and acknowledged, but rather than regarding it as formative and constructive, it is seen as summative at best and as criticism at worst. Even formative feedback along the lines of, "This is what you need to do to improve …" is often received as, "This is what you're not doing and the reason why you're not improving." For this learner, feedback is simply a statement about what they are unable or unwilling to do.

PERFORMANCE LEARNERS

Performance Learners are all about doing things well, to the peak of their ability. They **avoid** making mistakes by only doing tasks they know they will complete well. They remain in their Performance and Comfort Zones, where they know the Learning Landscape well and can minimise the chance of mistakes occurring.

When Performance Learners receive feedback, they tend to **select** the feedback that reinforces their abilities and performance. They will choose to look at the things they got right instead of the things they got wrong. They will accept positive affirmations and confirmation of their abilities but may put aside or brush off constructive and formative feedback designed to improve performance.

These learners like to have what they can do reaffirmed rather than pay attention to what they can do to improve.

DIRECTED LEARNERS

Directed Learners **correct** mistakes and **respond** to feedback.

As we've seen before, Directed Learners mostly do what they are directed to do. They are not proactive learners; they do not take charge of their own learning. Instead, they respond to directions given to them. These learners correct mistakes when they are

THE LEARNING LANDSCAPE

told how, but without specific direction, errors are likely to persist, and their growth will slow or halt.

Directed Learners respond to feedback but prefer specific directions. These learners don't do much "working it out for themselves". They are reactive to the teacher's direction and instructions.

Directed Learners consume a lot of the teacher's time, needing to be shown each step through a Challenge Pit, particularly when it is a Learning Challenge.

INDEPENDENT LEARNERS

Independent Learners **use** mistakes and **request** feedback.

When Independent Learners make mistakes, they are quick to react. Unlike the Directed Learner, who waits for others to identify their mistakes and tell them what to do, Independent Learners have a clear picture of what the Far Side of the Challenge Pit looks like and know when their performance falls short. They also take steps to get back on track.

When mistakes occur, Independent Learners analyse the mistake and look for what they can learn from it. If the mistake is unhelpful (they can't discern the information in it) the Independent Learner will seek other sources of feedback so they can continue to move forward.

AGILE LEARNERS

Agile Learners **design** mistakes and **tailor** feedback.

These learners are much more focused on the learning process than other learners. So, as they enter a challenge, they anticipate their mistakes. As a result, they carefully plot their path through a Challenge Pit, so that any mistakes made will produce the most helpful information. They seek to control their learning environment as much as possible to ensure any mistakes are highly informative.

Agile Learners know themselves as a learner and can anticipate the sort of feedback they are likely to require. They will tailor and proactively seek ways to gather feedback that best informs their learning. For example, they will ensure appropriate data is gathered so it can be used after mistakes occur. Or they might seek experts who are best placed to give them feedback and ask them to observe their performance. These learners anticipate what is likely to go wrong and prepare for it.

CHAPTER 5: PRACTICE

The critical difference between the Agile Learner and the Independent Learner is that the Agile Learner anticipates mistakes and the need for specific feedback. The Independent Learner responds to the need when it arises. Agile Learners are proactive. Independent learners are more reactive.

TEACHER ACTION: GUIDING THE CLIMB

Help students recognise that struggle and mistakes are a normal part of the learning process. They are to be expected when they are in their Learning Zone.

Teach students to recognise the difference between Productive and Unproductive Struggle, and what to do when they are in Unproductive Struggle.

The key to getting out of any struggle is information. Ensure students recognise mistakes and feedback as sources of information — not criticism — that can help them climb out of the Challenge Pit.

Ensure students recognise that mistakes (or other gaps) represent the start of learning, not the end of learning.

Ensure students understand the different types of mistakes described in this chapter. Help them recognise stretch mistakes as being a valuable part of the learning process.

To counter the common negative view of mistakes, teach students to recognise mistakes as one more way to help them recognise the gap between where they are now and where they want to be in the Learning Landscape. Mistakes are no different from a problem or an expert pointing out where their learning journey will take them.

Using the descriptions of how different learners respond to mistakes and feedback, ask students to identify the type of learner they are in this regard. Ask them what they might do to become a better learner.

Try to avoid praising mistakes. Instead, praise students for their positive learning behaviours. Praise them for being in their Learning Zone. Praise them for taking on Learning Challenges. Praise them for recognising Unproductive Struggle and seeking help. Praise them for recognising what the mistake told them. Most importantly, praise them for doing all of this and eventually fixing the mistake and getting out of a Challenge Pit.

CAROL DWECK: MINDSETS

Carol Dweck is the Lewis and Virginia Eaton Professor of Psychology at Stanford University. Her career, spanning more than 45 years, has seen her teach at Columbia University, Harvard University and the University of Illinois. Today, she is best known for her elucidation of the concept of mindset, which she describes in her landmark book, *Mindset: The New Psychology of Success* (2006).

Dweck's work describes the importance of learners' beliefs about their abilities. For example, when learners believe their abilities are fixed traits – things they are born with and unable to change significantly – they tend to avoid challenges and give up easily. On the other hand, when learners believe their basic abilities, talents and intelligence are malleable and can be developed through practice and effort, they are more likely to persist, listen and respond to feedback, and take on greater challenges.

In short, Dweck has shown that what a learner believes about their most basic characteristics affects how they approach learning. Learners with a Growth Mindset tend to adopt more positive learning behaviours. Learners with a Fixed Mindset tend to adopt less productive learning behaviours.

Importantly, Dweck has shown it is possible to change a learner's mindset, leading them to adopt more positive learning behaviours.

Dweck's work contributes to our metaphor of the Learning Landscape in two broad ways. Firstly, it helps us understand the behaviour of some learners. Learners with a Fixed Mindset build imaginary boundaries around themselves, limiting where they can go in the Learning Landscape. On the other hand, learners with a Growth Mindset understand they are free to travel anywhere in the Learning Landscape. Secondly, it helps students better understand themselves as learners. Rather than looking inside themselves to discover their abilities, they come to understand they are responsible for "filling their backpacks" and becoming better learners. Instead of looking around themselves to discover whether they are standing on top of a mountain of expertise, they realise they must climb to the top of that mountain via their own efforts.

The metaphor of the Learning Landscape helps develop a Growth Mindset in learners.

CHAPTER 6
MINDSET

A learner with a Growth Mindset understands the Learning Landscape. They know they can change their most basic characteristics – such as their talents, abilities and intelligence – by filling their backpack and becoming better climbers.

On the other hand, a learner with a Fixed Mindset believes they are born with limits to their abilities. They believe there are parts of the Learning Landscape that will forever be inaccessible to them and that no amount of effort will allow them to explore. These limits might be vertical and prevent them from going higher, or they might be horizontal and prevent them from venturing into particular parts of the Learning Landscape. These learners act as if there are boundaries around them.

While there is no direct relationship between learner types and mindset, they are interrelated. The effect of developing a Growth Mindset is to help students increase Learner Agency and become better learners more quickly.

Beginning Learners with a Growth Mindset are likely to become better learners more quickly. Conversely, a Fixed Mindset will hinder their development as a learner.

There is a significant relationship to note between experiencing growth and developing a Growth Mindset. The more effective people are as learners, the more they will experience growth and the more they will come to understand their ability to grow. This is likely to lead to a Growth Mindset. Conversely, ineffective, Below-the-Line Learners do not experience growth regularly, which is likely to lead to a Fixed Mindset.

THE LEARNING LANDSCAPE

ABOUT MINDSETS

The work shared here is an application and extension of the ground-breaking work of Professor Carol Dweck. Although Dweck did not invent the Growth Mindset, she identified it and has elucidated its importance to Learner Agency and learner success.

As previously stated, your mindset reflects the way you view your most basic characteristics: your talents, abilities and intelligence. The learner who recognises they are in charge of these characteristics and capable of developing them through their efforts is said to have a Growth Mindset. This learner understands they are responsible for filling their backpack. They recognise that they need to respond to mistakes and feedback to improve and to set themselves Learning Challenges so that they can climb higher in the Learning Landscape. This learner understands they are in control of their Learner Agency and can strive to become a better learner.

The learner who believes their characteristics are fixed is said to have a Fixed Mindset. They see their backpack as static – something to be drawn upon but that is not within their control to fill. The learner with a Fixed Mindset sees no way to improve their Learner Agency.

There is no direct relationship between learner type and mindset. It's not that Non-Learners have a Fixed Mindset (although they might) and Agile Learners have a Growth Mindset (although they are more likely to). Mindset affects Learner Agency by encouraging learners to take actions that will help them develop as a learner.

But as we will explore, a Growth Mindset is just a learner's belief in their ability to develop their talents, abilities and intelligence. This is not the same as having the capacity to develop these basic characteristics. So, understanding one's self as a learner and being an effective learner are often two different things.

SYMPTOMS OF MINDSET

The beliefs learners hold about their capacity to change lead them to make certain choices about their learning behaviours. We can think of these behaviours as being the symptoms of the learner's mindset – the outward signs of their inner beliefs. These behaviours have a significant impact on Learner Agency.

We use the term "symptom" to separate the cause from the effect. The underlying cause of the behaviour is the set of beliefs a learner holds about their abilities. What we see are their behaviours. But a mindset is not a set of behaviours; it's a set of

CHAPTER 6: MINDSET

beliefs. As we'll explore throughout this chapter, the distinction between beliefs and behaviours is critical in understanding the influence of mindset on growth, and on how we can change a learner's mindset.

In the context of the Learning Landscape, learners with a Fixed Mindset believe some people are born in the mountains, their backpacks already filled. They believe the differences they see between learners today are permanent. They think who they are determines what they'll be able to do. These learners have no concept of the importance of the backstory in the development of their abilities and achievements.

Someone with a fixed view of their abilities avoids challenges. They believe their "line" in the Learning Landscape is a predetermined limit beyond which they can never climb – a limit fixed at birth. To this person, a challenge – something that might put them in their Learning Zone – holds the prospect of almost certain failure. Consequently, they avoid challenges and frequently become Below-the-Line Learners.

Because learners with a Fixed Mindset see their abilities as limited, they give up easily. To them, struggling is a sign they have reached their limits. They believe all tasks should feel like Downhill Challenges – easy and within their ability. They believe that what is hard today will be hard tomorrow, so there's no point persisting with difficult tasks. These learners don't understand the difference between their Comfort Zone and their Learning Zone. They don't understand that every time they venture into their Learning Zone, it is meant to feel hard.

Effort and struggle are considered bad for someone with a Fixed Mindset. For them, effort is something that makes up for a deficit. If you had the ability, it would be easy, so effort is a sign they don't have that ability rather than a process through which they acquire the ability. For these learners, struggle is almost always unproductive.

From this learner's perspective, when they are recognised or praised for putting in effort, they feel they are having their deficits highlighted. It's the equivalent of being told, "I can see you *have* to put in all that effort, so you mustn't be very smart. If you were smart, you wouldn't have to put in so much effort." Effort becomes a sign of weakness. Consequently, these learners often seek to hide effort, or minimise the amount of effort they are perceived to put into a challenge.

These learners will frequently ignore feedback, regardless of whether it comes from an internal source, such as a mistake, or an external source, such as a teacher. From this learner's perspective, feedback isn't useful. They believe they can't improve, so feedback highlights their deficits. As a result, they choose not to listen to feedback.

THE LEARNING LANDSCAPE

Learners with a Fixed Mindset are also threatened by the success of others. They feel that other people's success makes them look bad, as it highlights a permanent deficit in their abilities and achievements. They think they will forever be looking up at the successful people who live in the mountains of the Learning Landscape.

SYMPTOMS OF THE GROWTH MINDSET

Someone with a Growth Mindset understands the Learning Landscape and themselves as a learner. They recognise they have been developing their abilities through their own efforts all their lives and are capable of continuing to build those abilities. These learners recognise the importance of filling their backpacks to succeed at increasingly difficult goals. They understand that what they do determines who they are, and they get on with learning how to do it even better. These learners have a keen understanding of the importance of the backstory.

Learners with a Growth Mindset embrace their Learning Zone. They are interested in Learning Challenges – challenges that help them grow. Downhill Challenges are mostly considered a waste of time. Why spend time doing more when you could spend it getting better?

These learners are persistent. They understand what is difficult today will become easy tomorrow. They recognise that as they stretch themselves and fill their backpacks, the things that were once difficult become easy. They want to make those hard things easy, so are more inclined to persist.

Learners with a Growth Mindset value effort as the driver of their growth. They know that any standard they are at today is where they are, not who they are. They understand their best is only their best when they measure it against yesterday's standard. By tomorrow's standard, it will be their second best. So, they are far more focused on what they are doing to improve their standard and climb higher in the Learning Landscape – their effort – than the standard they happen to be at today. Although these learners like reaching new standards, it's their backstory of how they got there and how they'll move onto even higher ground that they recognise as most important.

These learners love feedback. They understand that gaps in their abilities today are temporary. All they need is more information to close these gaps. So, they seek and use feedback to improve.

CHAPTER 6: MINDSET

Importantly, these learners embrace the success of others. They recognise they can learn from other people's success. Far from highlighting a deficit, these learners recognise that others' success shows them what's possible. Moreover, recognising the backstory of other people's success — understanding that their success comes from what they did, not who they are — reinforces their understanding of what's necessary to achieve their own goals.

It's important to note that from the perspective of these different sets of beliefs, the actions these learners engage in make perfect sense. If you believe you can't grow much, why would you waste your time doing things you can't do? If you can't do it today, move on to something you can do — don't waste your time trying to do something you're not capable of doing. It's not that learners with a Fixed Mindset are naughty or lazy — they are simply working within their belief system.

From the perspective of the learner with a Growth Mindset, why would you give up? If there's something you can't do that you want to do, then take on the challenge, listen to the feedback and focus on becoming a better learner until you can do it.

THE MINDSET CONTINUUM[33]

Of course, there are not only two types of people in the world — those with a Fixed Mindset and those with a Growth Mindset. The dichotomy of Fixed and Growth Mindsets is a simplification. In the real world, there are very few people who could genuinely be described as having a Fixed Mindset. Likewise, there are very few people who could be genuinely be considered to have a Growth Mindset. In reality, most people lie somewhere between these two extremes on the Mindset Continuum.

Learners vary in their beliefs about how much they can change their abilities. Some believe they can change a lot, while others believe they can change only a little. Some believe they can change in some areas but not in others, or that they are limited in how much they can change.

As a reflection of this range of beliefs, we see a corresponding range of behaviours. For example, we don't see only two responses to a challenge — the Fixed Mindset response to avoid it and the Growth Mindset response to embrace it. Instead, we see various responses in between. For example, some people may embrace only easy, Downhill Challenges, but will be inclined to shy away from more difficult Learning Challenges.

The Mindset Continuum (see Figure 11: The Mindset Continuum) describes the behaviours we see from learners on the low to high ends of the Mindset Continuum.

THE LEARNING LANDSCAPE

Figure 11: The Mindset Continuum.

Source: *The Agile Learner: Where Growth Mindset, Habits of Mind and Practice Unite.*
By James Anderson. Melbourne, VIC: Hawker Brownlow Education © 2017. Reproduced with Permission.

CHAPTER 6: MINDSET

Many learners might be better described as having a "limited Growth Mindset". They understand they are capable of learning new things and changing, but believe they are limited in how much they can change.

As we saw in *Chapter 2: Learners*, many learners limit themselves to growth in just one or two areas of the Learning Landscape. This is because of their mindset. These learners believe they can only develop and improve at, say, maths and science, but could never be good at music or art. In this way, they create imaginary fences for themselves in the Learning Landscape.

The tragedy of these self-imposed boundaries is that they limit the learner's choices in life. The learner who creates fences around themselves believes that parts of the Learning Landscape are forever out of their reach. They believe that, even if they wanted to, they could never explore certain parts of the Learning Landscape.

Similarly, as we also saw in *Chapter 2: Learners*, many learners limit themselves vertically in the Learning Landscape. They define a particular level of difficulty, a specific contour line they can never go above. They believe they are only smart enough to climb to a certain height, and that some problem levels are too difficult for "someone like them" to solve. It's as if they believe their backpack cannot hold anything more.

Again, this learner limits the choices they make in life. They believe they don't have the choice to take on something difficult because they simply don't have, and can't acquire, the abilities to succeed at that level of difficulty. As a result, even if they wanted to succeed at something more difficult, they believe they can't and so will never attempt the more challenging task.

To improve Learner Agency, we need to ensure learners develop an increasingly growth-oriented mindset. To understand how we change a learner's mindset, we need to first explore the relationship between a learner's experience of growth and the development of a Growth Mindset. We will then look at other factors that act as Mindset Movers to change a learner's mindset.

GROWTH MINDSET AND GROWTH

It is important to recognise that learners had mindsets before the term was coined. Professor Dweck did not invent mindsets; rather, she described the beliefs people held about themselves as learners and how these beliefs affected them. She then created the terms Fixed Mindset and Growth Mindset to (broadly) describe those beliefs.

THE LEARNING LANDSCAPE

This raises the interesting question of where those beliefs came from in the first place. How did anyone develop what we might term an "*authentic* Growth Mindset" before there was someone around to tell them it was a good idea? (We will compare authentic and learned Growth Mindsets below).

GROWTH AND THE GROWTH MINDSET

There is an important relationship between the experience of growth and the Growth Mindset. Experiencing growth leads to a Growth Mindset. Conversely, not experiencing growth leads to a Fixed Mindset.

Consider Figure 12: Emotional Cascade of the Fixed Mindset. As we've mentioned in the previous two chapters, at one time or another, most learners experience growth like this. They begin learning something new. What they are learning is just an "easy thing they haven't done yet". They already have some tools in their backpack and some prior knowledge, so the challenge is a Downhill Challenge. They progress quickly through the basics.

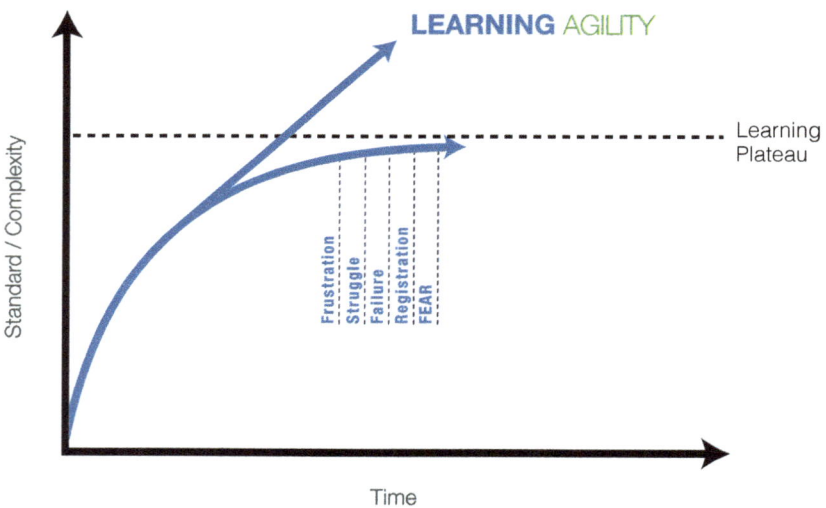

Figure 12: Emotional Cascade of the Fixed Mindset.

Source: *The Agile Learner: Where Growth Mindset, Habits of Mind and Practice Unite.*
By James Anderson. Melbourne, VIC: Hawker Brownlow Education © 2017. Reproduced with Permission.

But learners soon reach a point where the work becomes truly challenging. They pass through their Performance Zone, where the difficulty of the task matches their abilities, then into their Learning Zone. Progress becomes increasingly challenging and slows.

CHAPTER 6: MINDSET

As progress slows, learners feel frustrated and they struggle. If this struggle remains unproductive, they begin to fail and get stuck at the bottom of the pit. Continued failure leads to a sense of resignation, a feeling that they are "just not very good at this" and will never be able to get out of the pit. Too many learners experience learning this way. When Unproductive Struggle continues, learners expect failure and develop a fear of taking on similar challenges.

This fear is the Fixed Mindset. It is the fear of jumping into a pit and taking on Learning Challenges. It is the result of the learners' own lived experience that they have tried this sort of task before and have struggled and failed. Their experience tells them they were unable to complete this sort of challenge. They had put in the effort, and it wasn't enough. They were unable to succeed. So, they stop taking on the challenge as it represents only struggle and failure. It's a perfectly sensible thing to do in the face of the apparent evidence of their inability.

Of course, this is not always the way learning progresses. Consider Figure 13: Emotional Cascade of the Growth Mindset. If learners encounter difficulties and their focus is not only on what they are learning but also on how they are becoming better learners, they can have an entirely different experience. Learners who are taught how to develop their abilities, fill their backpacks with increasingly well-developed Habits of Mind, extract information from mistakes and respond to feedback will see continued growth and progress, even as the tasks become challenging.

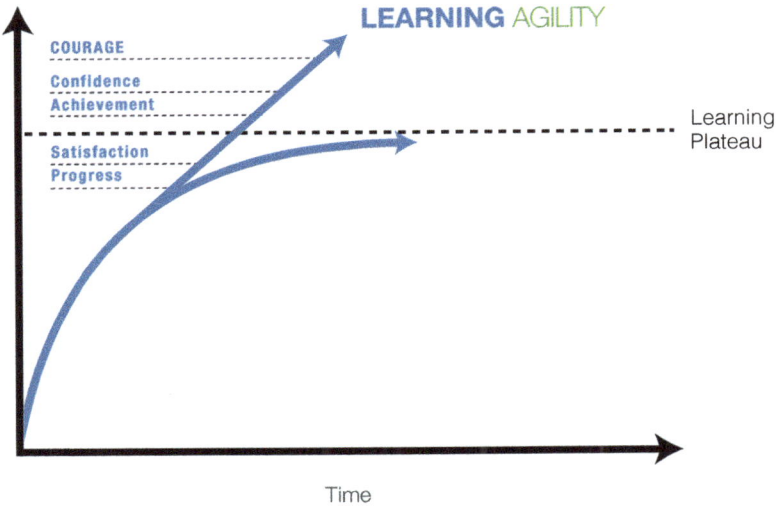

Figure 13: Emotional Cascade of the Growth Mindset.

Source: *The Agile Learner: Where Growth Mindset, Habits of Mind and Practice Unite.*
By James Anderson. Melbourne, VIC: Hawker Brownlow Education © 2017. Reproduced with Permission.

101

THE LEARNING LANDSCAPE

As learners experience progress, they develop a very different set of beliefs about themselves as learners. They gain a sense of satisfaction. As they move beyond their previous limits, they begin to feel a sense of achievement. They build confidence and, eventually, a sense of courage.

In a very real sense, the Growth Mindset is the Courage Mindset. A learner's own experience of having taken on challenges that were beyond their previous abilities, and to have succeeded, teaches them the reality that they are capable of growth. This gives them the courage to jump into a Challenge Pit and take on Learning Challenges when they don't immediately know how they'll succeed. They've done that before and learned that by focusing on how they learn, they can become more capable.

LEARNED AND AUTHENTIC GROWTH MINDSETS

It is important to note that for an authentic Growth Mindset, the experience of growth led to the learner's development of a Growth Mindset. When learners are taught how to overcome difficulties, they experience the growth that results. They learn firsthand they are capable of developing themselves as learners, and their experiences directly affect their beliefs about themselves as learners. We then recognise those beliefs as a Growth Mindset.

But in many schools, the approach is to teach learners that they are capable of growth before they have done the hard work and achieved growth. This is what we might describe as a "learned Growth Mindset". It is a promise made to learners that they are capable of growth.

It is one thing to say growth leads to a Growth Mindset. It is an entirely different thing to suggest that a Growth Mindset will lead to growth. A Growth Mindset is the belief you are capable of growth, but it is not the capacity to achieve that growth. That capacity comes from learning how to engage in the right actions.

This is why there are people who have learned about the Growth Mindset but remain unable to grow. They have accepted the promise they are capable of growth, they repeat the catchphrases, but they lack the understanding of how to achieve the growth.

Growth Mindset catchphrases such as "believe and you'll achieve" are misleading. To grow, the learner must engage in the right sort of actions – actions we have explored in the past few chapters. It would be more accurate to say, "Believe and you'll act. Act effectively and you'll achieve."

CHAPTER 6: MINDSET

Belief is important. It gives learners the courage to act. But on its own, belief is not enough. To achieve, learners also need capacity, and that's something that must be learned.

How learners developed a Growth or Fixed Mindset before we had a term to describe these beliefs, and why a Growth Mindset does not guarantee growth, gives us our first insight into more effective methods of developing Growth Mindsets in our schools and classrooms. But these methods are not what most schools are using to develop Growth Mindsets today.

CHANGING MINDSETS

Recall that a mindset is a set of *beliefs* the learner has about their ability to grow. To grow, the learner must take *action*. They need to take on Learning Challenges, fill their backpack with well-developed Habits of Mind and engage in the right sort of practice to turn Unproductive Struggle into Productive Struggle. Furthermore, how the learner *experiences* growth, or a lack of it, feeds back into their beliefs about themselves.

In this way, there are three elements to consider if we want to change mindsets and help learners achieve growth: beliefs, actions and experiences (see Figure 14: Beliefs, Actions and Experiences.).

Figure 14: Beliefs, Actions and Experiences.

103

THE LEARNING LANDSCAPE

BELIEFS AND THE IGNORANCE PROBLEM

One of the most common approaches to changing a learner's mindset is to simply change their beliefs. This approach addresses what we call the "Ignorance Problem" and develops the *learned* Growth Mindset. Learners don't know how much growth they are capable of, so the theory goes if the teacher tells them they are capable of change, then everything will be okay!

This approach leads to slogans, catchphrases and affirmations designed to encourage learners to believe in themselves. Posters are prominently displayed in classrooms, saying, "Don't say you can't! Say you can't, YET!" Teachers tell learners about their amazing plastic brain and how it rewires itself with learning. Social media is full of this sort of stuff. Most of it is accurate in its own way, but equally, most of it is incomplete as it does not tell learners how to achieve that growth. As we've already pointed out, believing you can achieve is not the same as achieving.

All these slogans and affirmations do is encourage learners to take action. Taking action is a necessary first step, but ultimately, whether or not learners achieve growth is down to their next steps – the specific actions they take. If they take the right sort of actions by taking on Learning Challenges, filling their backpacks with well-developed Habits of Mind and responding to feedback, then it is likely they will achieve growth and the teacher's promise will be fulfilled.

But many of the learners we target with these slogans and affirmations – the learners with a Fixed Mindset – don't know which actions they should take. Strategies that target the Ignorance Problem get learners to take the first step into a Challenge Pit but do little to show them what to do when they are in there. They don't know what actions to take for their next steps!

This is a problem because by using slogans and catchphrases, the teacher makes a promise to the learner. They promise the learner they will grow. But if the teacher does not show them how to achieve that growth, their promise will be broken. The learner will again experience failure. And it is this experience that feeds back into the learner's belief system. Faced with a choice of believing the teacher, whose promise has gone unfulfilled, or believing their own experience of having not succeeded, the more powerful influence is likely to be the learner's lived experience. Not only has the student not succeeded, they are also likely to have lost trust in their teacher as well.

CHAPTER 6: MINDSET

ACTIONS AND THE EFFICACY PROBLEM

Believing you can grow is not enough. Learners also need to be taught how to grow, and that's the job of the teacher. Telling learners they are capable of growth only addresses the Ignorance Problem. Teaching them the right actions – the ones that will truly develop their abilities, including how to successfully negotiate Challenge Pits that represent Learning Challenges, develop their Habits of Mind and practise in the right way – addresses what we call the "Efficacy Problem".

The reason why many learners fail to grow, and the reason why they may have developed a Fixed Mindset, is because their actions have not been effective, so they experienced failure. That sense of learned failure has been their real, lived experience. In the past, they have put in the effort, they have persisted, they have tried to climb out of a Challenge Pit, but their efforts have gone unrewarded. Their struggle remained unproductive. In short, they have been left at the bottom of the pit, not experiencing the growth that comes from climbing out.

Most of this book has focused on the Efficacy Problem. We have looked at how to increase Learner Agency by helping learners understand the nature of the Learning Landscape. We've distinguished Learning Challenges from other sorts of challenges. We've explored how to equip learners by filling their backpacks with mature Habits of Mind. And we've discussed how to engage in "the climb" using feedback and mistakes to inform their journey. If we focus solely on building Learner Agency, learners are likely to experience growth and so develop an authentic Growth Mindset.

Do we need to teach learners about Growth Mindset? Possibly not. There is good evidence that teaching learners about mindset helps them become more metacognitive – more reflective of their behaviours – and that's a good thing. But I am wary of "teaching" Growth Mindset to learners, as it tends to lead educators down the path of focusing on the topic of mindset without concentrating on how to achieve growth.

EXPERIENCE AND THE PERCEPTION PROBLEM

As we've seen, possibly the most important influence on a learner's mindset is their experience of growth. For learners to develop an authentic Growth Mindset, they must experience growth. When learners recognise the changes in their abilities and the associated increases in standards, they know firsthand that they are capable of growth.

105

THE LEARNING LANDSCAPE

It would be easy to think that simply telling learners they are capable of growth, and teaching them how to grow, would be enough. But this is not necessarily the case. Achieving growth is not the same as experiencing it.

For example, consider the story of Rohan.

Rohan was a Year 7 student struggling with maths. He didn't consider himself very good at it. In fact, he thought he couldn't do maths at all. One day, out of frustration, he threw his books across the table, yelling, "I can't do maths!" The teacher, after helping Rohan calm down, challenged him on his statement. The teacher asked, "What if I gave you Year 6 maths, could you do Year 6 maths?"

Sitting a bit straighter in his chair, Rohan replied, "Yeah! I can do Year 6 maths. Year 6 maths is easy!"

"So, it's not that you can't do maths then, Rohan. It's just that you haven't learned how to do this maths yet. Is that right?", the teacher asked.

The question confused Rohan. In his mind, he couldn't do maths, but the teacher had just pointed out he could do Year 6 maths. It was easy.

Reflect for a moment on Rohan's experience in his maths lessons. In Year 1, he had been below standard. He had learned and improved. But he had stayed behind the standard of the other students in his class. When he went to Year 2, although he was now at a higher standard, he was still described as "below standard". He had improved, but his teachers had moved the "standard" on him, so he was still below standard. In fact, despite constant growth, Rohan was always "below standard". The school system used the same term to describe different standards, so Rohan never experienced his growth!

To Rohan, he was the dumbest kid in the world when it came to maths! Because his world consisted of 25 other students, the system kept moving along with him, whenever he looked around, he was at the bottom of the pile. In short, the school system kept moving all of Rohan's measuring sticks, so despite achieving considerable growth, he never recognised this growth. In his mind, he really couldn't do maths.

But Rohan could do maths. In his own words, "Year 6 maths was easy." He had grown considerably in his abilities over the past six years and had increased in standard – quite possibly, just as much as any other student in the room. He had been achieving one year's growth in one year's time, but he had been consistently one year behind the other students in his year level – so Rohan didn't recognise or experience his growth.

CHAPTER 6: MINDSET

It is not enough that learners grow – they must also recognise this growth. In Rohan's case, he had been described as "below standard" so often that he had come to believe it was a description of who he was, not where he was. As we've stated many times previously, standards are where you are, not who you are. Rohan had been climbing higher in the Learning Landscape; he had just never been given the opportunity to recognise this growth.

Roger Federer understands this problem (see the story of McEnroe versus Federer at the end of this chapter). He says that "staying the same is like going backwards".[34] That's because in the world of competitive tennis, everyone is always improving. The overall standard goes up and up. Everyone learns from everyone else, and every player climbs higher in the Learning Landscape.

Federer recognises that only being as good as he was last year means that, comparatively, he's going backwards. He knows that to maintain his ranking, he must continuously improve. He experiences his growth by recognising the improvement in his standard of play (fewer errors, hitting better shots, etc.). We saw a similar story with Nadia Comăneci, who was a great gymnast. But compared to today's standards, her 1976 Olympic standard would not be considered very good.

The point here is that learners must not only grow, they must also experience their growth. When they fail to experience their growth, they suffer from the "Perception Problem".

Many common school practices create the Perception Problem. Among these practices is using the same name to describe different standards. For example, a B grade in Year 4 is not the same as a B grade in Year 5, but many learners believe they are still at a B, or worse, they get a C in Year 5 and think they have gone backwards. Normative assessment, which compares learners to other learners in the cohort, can also create the Perception Problem. The entire cohort might have moved forward significantly, but recognition is given only to ranking compared to other learners.

Of course, there is another sort of Perception Problem. This one arises from perceiving growth when there is none. This frequently happens for Below-the-Line Learners. These learners may be learning new things, but they aren't learning harder things – they aren't becoming better learners. This problem might also occur when teachers give learners many Downhill or Performance Challenges – easy tasks – often with the intent of boosting confidence. The trouble with this approach is that this below-the-line "success" builds fragile confidence in a learner's abilities. When the learner eventually encounters their Learning Zone, they are not prepared and consequently run a greater risk of failure. This new experience is likely to lead to the sort of "Limited Growth Mindset" we discussed above.

THE LEARNING LANDSCAPE

What matters most is not how learners compare to other learners, but rather how they compare to where they were at the start of the unit of work. Even more important are the actions they took to achieve that growth or what they are doing to create their backstory. Ultimately, the standard the learner is at is temporary. It is sometimes important and/or necessary to rank and compare learners, but as educators, we must ensure learners can perceive their real growth and the actions that lead them to improve.

THE FIVE Fs OF PRACTICE

One way to help learners perceive their growth is to apply the "5 Fs of Practice". In *Chapter 5: Practice*, we explored Anders Ericsson's "3 Fs of Practice": Focus, Feedback and Fix It. To help learners recognise their growth, we will extend Ericsson's 3 Fs to ensure learners can see where they are starting and how much they have changed.

- **Focus 1:** Recognise the Near Side of the Challenge Pit. What are your current standards and abilities? What can and can't you currently do?
- **Focus 2:** Recognise the Far Side of the Challenge Pit. What are you trying to achieve? How will you know when it's been achieved?
- **Feedback:** Get feedback on your progress. How close are you to your goal?
- **Fix It:** Make corrections and adjustments. Get out of the pit!
- **Finish:** Recognise how far you've come. Turn around, recognise the journey. Enjoy the view from the new part of the Learning Landscape. Celebrate what can you do now that you couldn't do before.

Helping learners recognise their growth is an example of a Mindset Mover. Mindset Movers are actions teachers take that influence a learner's mindset. Positive Mindset Movers tend to push learners towards the growth end of the Mindset Continuum. Negative Mindset Movers push them towards the fixed end. As educators, we want to increase Learner Agency and help learners become better. So, it is essential we examine our practice to increase the number of Positive Mindset Movers and decrease the number of Negative Mindset Movers.

WHY IT'S EASIER TO CATCH A FIXED MINDSET THAN A GROWTH MINDSET

The things we say – the messages we send to learners – act directly on their beliefs. This is why it's much easier to "catch" a Fixed Mindset than a Growth Mindset. To create a Fixed Mindset is a one-step process. All you need to do is change a learner's beliefs about their ability.

CHAPTER 6: MINDSET

To create a Growth Mindset is a three-step process. You need to change learners' beliefs, as well as their actions, and ensure they experience the growth that results.

The reason for this is if what we say to learners gives them fixed messages about their abilities, they become self-fulfilling prophecies. For example, consider the learner who is told, "You're just not very good at maths." If they believe this, they'll probably stop doing maths or at least not put in as much effort. Not doing maths is a sure-fire way of not getting better at it! When this learner doesn't experience growth in their mathematical abilities, they'll have their beliefs confirmed. The Fixed Mindset does not have an Efficacy Problem.

Ericsson makes this same point when discussing people's ability (or inability) to sing.[35] He points out that the number-one reason why most people can't sing (well) is that at some point in their lives, someone told them they couldn't sing. From that point on, they did not practise and never got any better!

In trying to develop a Growth Mindset in learners, we need to move beyond telling them simply to believe in themselves. We must also focus on how they can achieve that growth. Learner Agency ultimately comes from action. Beliefs simply fuel those actions.

But it is possible for a Directed Learner, or even an Independent Learner, to engage in the actions that will lead them to growth, even if they have a Fixed Mindset. They will still grow but may believe it was a result of their innate abilities. This is why Dweck can point to many high-achieving individuals with a Fixed Mindset. The Growth Mindset is not required for growth, but it helps!

TEACHER ACTION: MINDSET MOVERS

The entire metaphor of the Learning Landscape and associated ideas discussed in this book will help contribute to the development of a Growth Mindset.

Help students recognise the symptoms of the Fixed Mindset and challenge them when they recognise these symptoms in themselves or others. For example, when a student says, "I can't do this," translate that into the language of the Learning Landscape and question why they can't. Is it because they need to fill their backpack? Is it because the challenge is an Aspirational Challenge outside their Learning Zone? Do they simply need more information to move forward? Ensure any temporary failure is attributed to what the learner is doing, not who they are, and direct them towards more efficacious behaviours.

THE LEARNING LANDSCAPE

Teach students about the Mindset Continuum and don't let any student label themselves as having a Growth Mindset or a Fixed Mindset. This will avoid stigma that is often attached to the Fixed Mindset. The question is always, how growth-oriented are they? How do they become more growth-oriented?

Reflect on your mindset as a teacher. Some of the most powerful influences on a learner's mindset are the subtle, often unconscious messages they receive from you as a teacher every day. Once you see the world through the Growth Mindset lens, you'll send many more Growth Mindset messages to your students.

MINDSET MOVERS

Mindset Movers are experiences teachers create that can have an impact on a student's mindset and, consequently, move them along the Mindset Continuum.

Mindset Movers can be positive, creating the opportunity for a more growth-oriented Mindset to develop, or they can be negative, pushing the learner towards the more fixed end of the Mindset Continuum.

Shifting learners' beliefs about themselves as learners is not a quick or straightforward task. It takes many Mindset Movers, over an extended period, before significant changes are likely to be seen.

It's also important to note that not all Mindset Movers are equal. Some will have more impact than others. Nor are they equal for all learners. Some will be affected by a Mindset Mover more than others.

As educators, we can only influence the Mindset Movers learners experience in schools. They will experience many more at home and in the community. It is important to remember that although we can't change these outside influences, a learner's mindset will ultimately be the result of the total of all of these Mindset Movers, so every Positive Mindset Mover we create, and every Negative Mindset Mover we eliminate, will contribute to an increasingly growth-oriented mindset for our learners.

All Mindset Movers will affect either a learner's beliefs, actions or experience of growth. Of these, the most important are likely to be the Mindset Movers that affect actions and experiences.

CHAPTER 6: MINDSET

In schools, it's useful to consider these Mindset Movers through the five broad areas outlined below. Please note that this is not a complete or exhaustive list. It is intended as a guide to common Mindset Movers in the classroom.

1. Learning
2. Effort
3. Mistakes and Feedback
4. Achievements
5. Narratives

The list below outlines the broad types of approaches that will act as positive or negative Mindset Movers.

NEGATIVE MINDSET MOVER	OUR LEARNING	POSITIVE MINDSET MOVER
Naive	Type	Virtuous
More	Result	Better

	OUR EFFORT	
Failure	Effect	Growth
Unproductive	Struggle	Productive
Cruising	Distribution	Effective Effort
Under/Over	Calibration	Accurate
Compensation	Impetus	Required

	OUR MISTAKES	
End Learning	Timing	Begin Learning
Good/Bad	Message	Signposts
Confuse	Information	Helpful
Low	Learning Potential	High
Risk	Emotion	Safe

	OUR ACHIEVEMENTS	
Categorise	Labels	Place on Continuum
Others	Comparators	Self
Better than Others	Successes	Better than Self
Hidden	Growth	Disclosed
Who You Are	Attribution	What you did

	OUR STORIES	
Machine	Brain	Plastic
Categorisation	Backstories	Specialisation
Being	Nature	Becoming
External/Destiny	Drivers	Free Will
Find	Motivation	Nurture

THE LEARNING LANDSCAPE

MCENROE VERSUS FEDERER

In her book, Mindset: The New Psychology of Success, *Professor Carol Dweck uses John McEnroe as an example of a person with a Fixed Mindset.[36] I think he's a great example for many reasons.*

You can't argue with the fact McEnroe was an extraordinary tennis player. He is ranked 6th in the list of most career match wins on the ATP World Tour – that's more than Andre Agassi, Novak Djokovic and Andy Murray. He is often considered among the greatest players in the history of tennis.

Dweck's use of McEnroe as an example of someone with a Fixed Mindset dispels the idea that only people with a Growth Mindset can grow. You don't need a Growth Mindset to grow – it just helps.

The Growth Mindset is the understanding that growth is possible. To achieve that growth, learners need to develop mature Habits of Mind and apply them through the process of Virtuous Practice. In the context of the Learning Landscape, learners need to fill their backpack and get on with the business of climbing mountains of expertise, traversing many Learning Challenges along the way. McEnroe didn't have a Growth Mindset, but he did develop many Habits of Mind and engage in Virtuous Practice, which led him to become one of the world's most successful tennis players.

The benefit of a Growth Mindset is it invites you to take these actions and guides your responses as you engage in the process. Think about what happened when McEnroe made a mistake – the tantrums and the dummy spits. Of course, it's natural to feel disappointed when we make mistakes, particularly when they happen in high-stakes situations. But in McEnroe's case, he directed his frustration outwards – at the umpire, the ball boy, the crowd – rather than directing his energy and attention inwards towards learning and improvement.

McEnroe's focus was always on protecting his appearance of being a great tennis player. He wanted to be seen standing on the highest peaks of the sport. If he wasn't having a great day or if he was losing a match, rather than accept responsibility and be accountable for his performance and what he needed to do to improve, he would blame someone else.

CHAPTER 6: MINDSET

McEnroe also didn't like to practise. He saw practice as a sign of weakness, that there might be something wrong with his game – something he couldn't admit. He was all about being better than other people.

Compare McEnroe to Roger Federer, who, in my opinion, is the quintessential Growth Mindset tennis player. Federer makes a point of practising harder than almost anyone else in the game – and he says so. For him, practice isn't a sign of weakness, it's a sign of commitment to his growth and becoming a better player.

Federer not only understands that he is capable of growth, but also how to go about achieving that growth. He has what is described as good "Motivation Calibration" – he recognises that Virtuous Practice is the price he must pay to improve.

Federer understands psychologist Anders Ericsson when he says, "What motivates the very best to practise so hard? They understand that such practise is essential to improving performance. That's it. Not because they love to practise. Because they love to improve."[37]

Federer is all about improvement. For him, mistakes aren't a sign of weakness. In many ways, they are a blessing because they help him home in on what he needs to work on to improve. He's not out to be the best in the world – he's out to be his best.

In some ways, I feel Federer doesn't compete against the other players so much as he uses them to improve his own game. When he does lose or make a mistake, he doesn't assign blame or make excuses. Rather, he praises his opponent for the way they played (noting there's something he can learn from them) and points to shortcomings he needs to work on.

I think Federer sums up his Growth Mindset attitude in this quote:

"I always questioned myself in the best of times, even when I was world number one for many, many weeks and months in a row, at certain times during the year I said, 'What can I improve? What do I need to change?' Because if you don't do anything or you just do the same thing over and over again, you stay the same, and staying the same means going backwards. It's important for me to actually hear criticism sometimes because I think that's what makes me a better player".[38]

THE LEARNING LANDSCAPE

I love the way he finishes that quote: "That's what makes me a better player." He's not particularly interested in being world number one. He wants to be the best player he can be. Even when he is world number one, he looks for ways to improve and push himself. When you focus on being better than yourself, your world ranking looks after itself.

Moreover, Federer's Growth Mindset is what makes him such a gracious player. Unlike McEnroe, Federer knows the game isn't about proving he's the best. It's not a measure of who he is. Rather, it's a recognition of the work he's done, a measure of where he is at and a way to continue to better himself.

A Growth Mindset is not a promise of growth; it is an invitation to grow. It gives you the understanding that you are capable of growth. It allows you to more deeply and effectively engage in the behaviours and processes required to achieve that growth. It's not essential to growth, but it helps – a lot!

WHY MANY GROWTH MINDSET INTERVENTIONS FAIL

This chapter would be incomplete if we didn't address a growing voice of criticism related to Growth Mindset. It's not that Dweck's ideas are being challenged; the challenges are directed at the interventions schools are implementing in an attempt to change students' mindsets. It turns out that many of them aren't working!

For example, one recent study that looked at the results of 273 school-based Growth Mindset interventions reported that these interventions "don't work most of the time", i.e. they did not significantly improve student learning outcomes.[40]

The reason why many Growth Mindset interventions aren't working is that educators have confused a Growth Mindset (a person's belief in their ability to grow) with growth – the actual improvement in student learning outcomes. These are two different things.

It is a mistake to assume that developing a Growth Mindset will automatically lead to higher standards. Any intervention that changes students' beliefs about themselves is an important first step towards improving student performance. But it is only the first step.

Changing learners' beliefs can only lead learners to make different choices about their actions. For example, instead of avoiding a challenge, they may choose to take on

CHAPTER 6: MINDSET

that challenge. Instead of giving up, they may choose to stick at a task for longer. But whether they succeed at that challenge will depend on the specific actions they take and how well prepared they are for the challenge, i.e. how full their backpack is.

Learners don't believe their way to higher standards. To achieve growth, learners must take the right sort of actions. They must develop mature Habits of Mind and engage these through the process of Virtuous Practice.

The trouble is that many schools seek to change results solely by addressing learners' beliefs. For example, they teach students that their brain is like a muscle and can grow. Or they tell learners not to say, "I can't," but instead to say, "I can't, yet." These interventions only address part of the problem. They seek to reassure students that they are capable of growth without taking the essential next step of building Learner Agency, so that they can achieve that growth.

Of course, for some students, these interventions will be enough. Shifting from the inaction of the Fixed Mindset to the action of the Growth Mindset will have an immediate benefit. These learners may already have reasonably well-developed Habits of Mind in their backpacks. Or the learner might engage in Productive Struggle, leading them to work it out on their own. In these cases, we will see improvements in student learning outcomes.

But many students will need support filling their backpacks and building Learner Agency before we see improvements in learning outcomes. This is why we need to see a shift in focus away from Mindset on its own towards Motivation Calibration.

Motivation Calibration is not only a measure of a student's understanding of their capacity to grow (their Growth Mindset) but also of their ability to accurately describe what actions they need to engage in to achieve that growth. Research by McKinsey and Company, using large data sets from PISA results in Africa and Europe, supports the idea that Motivation Calibration is a better predictor of student success than mindset alone.[41]

These findings make sense in light of our discussion of learner types and the Learning Landscape. Someone with good Motivation Calibration will be an Above-the-Line Learner. They understand they are free to move through the Learning Landscape. They also appreciate that this will require specific types of actions, including taking on Learning Challenges and filling their backpacks with well-developed Habits of Mind. They can "count the cost" of achieving growth.

Growth Mindset interventions will continue to fail to achieve significant increases in student learning outcomes unless they are simultaneously coupled with interventions that help build Learner Agency.

CHAPTER 7
EFFORT

Traditionally, effort has been considered a measure of the time and energy a learner puts into a task. In this chapter, we shift our focus to include not only the amount of time and energy spent, but also *how* they are spent. We look at whether learners spend their time and energy above or below the line, and whether they draw on their most well-developed Habits of Mind from their backpack.

We will explore four different types of effort: Low Effort, Performance Effort, Ineffective Effort and Effective Effort. We will also discover how different learners increase their Learner Agency by becoming increasingly adept at distributing their time between these different types of effort.

Recognising that not all effort is equal – that some types of effort are more efficacious than others – means teachers must rethink the way they perceive, reward, praise and value effort in the classroom. This requires a shift from thinking of effort as time and energy to focusing more on efficacy.

THE LEARNING LANDSCAPE

ABOUT EFFORT[39]

Moving around the Learning Landscape takes effort. Whether learners are going uphill or downhill, challenging themselves or cruising, as long as they're moving, they're expending time and energy.

But what does a learner gain from expending all that time and energy? Time and energy aren't of any value unless they have had some effect. Learners and educators need to ask, "What has been the net effect of spending all that time and energy?"

There's a big difference between a lesson spent producing and a lesson spent growing. Both take time and energy, but the net effect of the time spent growing is that the learner has gained height in the Learning Landscape and increased their Learner Agency by becoming a better climber. In short, the time spent growing had more effect — it was more efficacious.

Our traditional focus on time and energy shifts our attention away from the real goal of learning: efficacy. As a result, effort is sometimes used as a consolation prize in classrooms. We hear phrases like, "As long as you tried your hardest and put in the effort, then that's okay." Statements like this reward time and energy that have been spent without result, running counter to everything we've discussed about building Learner Agency and becoming better learners.

It is not "okay, as long as you've tried your hardest". If the way a learner spends their time and energy does not produce growth, then it's not because the learner is incapable of growth, it's because they spend their time and energy the wrong way!

Comments like this often suggest to the learner that they've done everything they can, but despite those efforts, they have not achieved. The message, therefore, is that they aren't capable of any better. They have found their limit or a part of the Learning Landscape they can't move through, and "at least they tried their hardest" is given as a consolation prize instead of the real goal of growth.

Throughout this book, we've stressed that success is not about who you are, it's about what you do. If the learner is not achieving success, then it's not because they are the wrong type of person, it's because they are doing the wrong things. It might be that they only set themselves Downhill Challenges, or they don't equip themselves sufficiently to climb out of the pit in a Learning Challenge. It might be that they are stuck in Ineffective Effort, failing to extract information from mistakes and feedback. In terms of effort, a learner who fails to see the growth we expect is likely to be engaging in the wrong sort of effort.

CHAPTER 7: EFFORT

We don't want our learners to merely put in effort — we want their effort to produce results. Our focus needs to be less on time and energy, and more on *efficacy*.

EFFECTIVE EFFORT MATRIX

The Effective Effort Matrix helps us distinguish four different types of effort (see Figure 15: Effective Effort Matrix.). Although all types of effort require the learner to spend time and energy, the effect of that time and energy varies greatly.

The Effective Effort Matrix divides effort into four types, based on *where* the learner spends their time and energy (above or below the line), and *how* that time and energy is spent (drawing on everything in their backpack, or just using some simple tools).

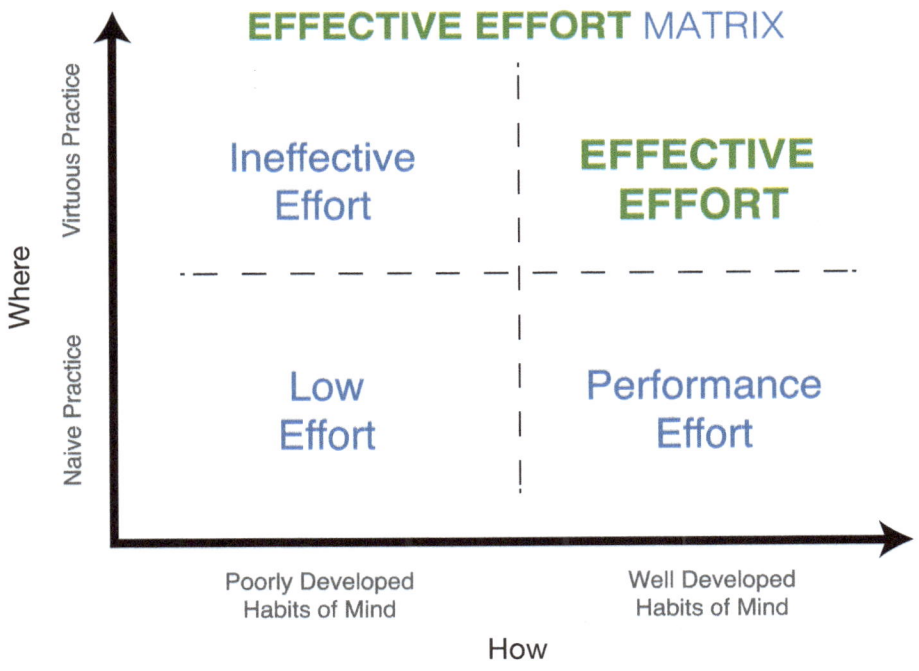

Figure 15: Effective Effort Matrix.

Source: *The Agile Learner: Where Growth Mindset, Habits of Mind and Practice Unite.*
By James Anderson. Melbourne, VIC: Hawker Brownlow Education 2017. Reproduced with Permission.

THE LEARNING LANDSCAPE

❶ LOW EFFORT: CRUISING

The learner engaged in Low Effort is cruising. They operate well below the line in their Comfort Zone. The challenges they take on are Downhill Challenges, so the climbing skills they call upon are well within their existing abilities.

There are times when everyone needs to engage in Low Effort. Some tasks don't demand much of us but need to get done. We have to add up the bill, send the email, answer the easy question. It's part of being alive and being an effective learner: some tasks are well within their abilities. These might be routine tasks the learner has done many times before, or they may be new "easy things they haven't done yet". Either way, they don't stretch the learner at all.

There is nothing wrong with Low Effort. The question is, how much time does the learner spend in Low Effort, and is that the wisest or more most effective way to spend that time?

❷ PERFORMANCE EFFORT: PERFORMING

The learner engaged in Performance Effort performs to the peak of their current abilities. The challenges they engage in are flat challenges that demand everything the learner has, but nothing more.

There are many times when it's appropriate to engage in Performance Effort. These are situations where errors are undesirable or possibly harmful. For example, doing a test is a performance situation, as is landing a Boeing 747. Both situations demand performances that are as error-free as possible.

Again, there are times when it is entirely appropriate to engage in Performance Effort. But there are some learners – Performance Learners, for example – who tend to engage in this sort of effort too frequently. Sometimes, instead of doing their best, learners should attempt to do better.

❸ INEFFECTIVE EFFORT: STRUGGLE

The learner engaged in Ineffective Effort is struggling. They are engaged in a Learning Challenge, but see little, if any, progress. This is due to either insufficiently developed Habits of Mind and/or engaging in an Aspirational Challenge.

CHAPTER 7: EFFORT

A sure sign a learner is engaged in Ineffective Effort is when the time and energy they spend on a task increases, but progress slows or stops. They are attempting to climb out of the Challenge Pit but repeatedly fall back down.

The struggle of Ineffective Effort is a natural part of the learning process. It is often the first sign a learner is stretching themselves and has entered their Learning Zone.

As we discussed in *Chapter 5: Practice*, the important part of this type of effort is that the learner uses the information generated by mistakes to gather feedback and shift the struggle into Productive Struggle.

Every learner experiences Ineffective Effort. The question is, how do they respond to it? Does the learner languish, failing to progress? Do they change what they are doing and drop back to Performance Effort or Low Effort? Or do they shift to Productive Struggle and make Effective Effort possible?

❹ EFFECTIVE EFFORT: GROWTH

As they learn from the struggle of Ineffective Effort, learners move into Ericsson's "Fix It" phase of practice. The learner applies their newly developed learning behaviours in their backpack to the task of climbing out of a Challenge Pit.

Counterintuitively, the shift from Ineffective Effort is characterised by a decrease in time and energy and an increase in the amount of growth achieved. Rather than sliding back down into the pit, the learner climbs out!

Learning situations demand Effective Effort. This sort of effort is the most efficacious. It is not that we want learners to be in this sort of effort all the time. Rather, we want learners to recognise when they should engage in it and to maximise their learning time in Effective Effort.

HOW DIFFERENT LEARNERS RESPOND TO EFFORT

Increasing Learner Agency is not as simple as asking learners to put in *more* effort. Nor is it a case of asking them to engage exclusively in Effective Effort. Each type of effort has its place. The most effective learners are best able to recognise the appropriate time and place for each sort of effort and distribute their time in the most efficacious way.

THE LEARNING LANDSCAPE

NON-LEARNERS

Non-Learners **waste** their effort. By not taking action, their time has little net effect (see Figure 16: Effort – Non-Learners.).

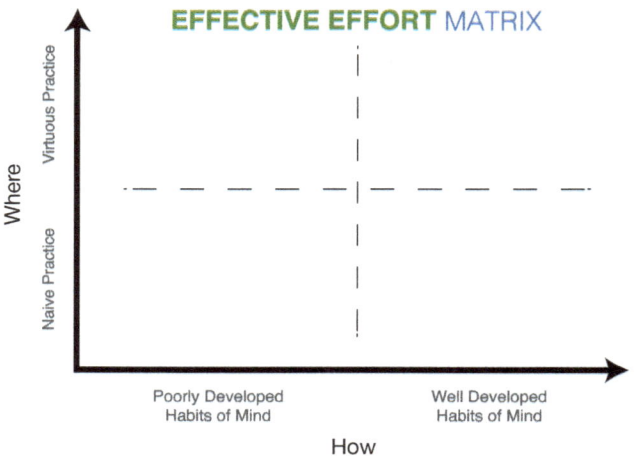

Figure 16: Effort – Non-Learners.

BEGINNING LEARNERS

Beginning Learners spend their effort in **doing** things. Being Below-the-Line Learners, the tasks they take on tend to be Downhill Challenges. When pushed, these learners will spend some time in Performance Effort but left to their own devices, they tend towards the bottom left of the Effective Effort Matrix (see Figure 17: Effort – Beginning Learners.).

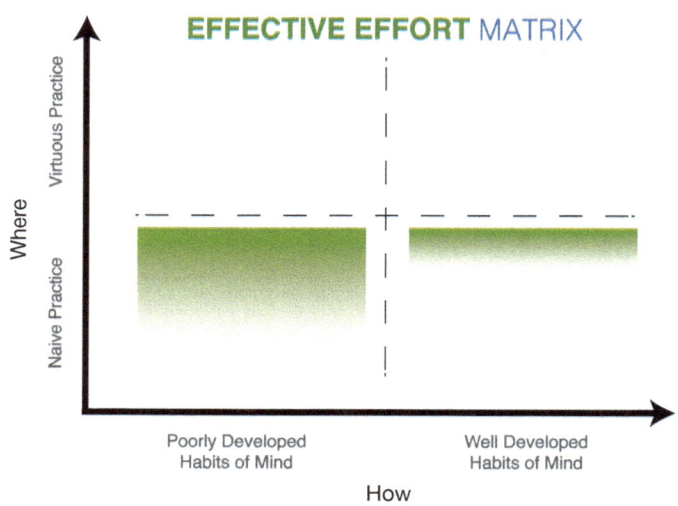

Figure 17: Effort – Beginning Learners.

CHAPTER 7: EFFORT

PERFORMANCE LEARNERS

Performance Learners spend their effort **performing**. They keep themselves at the peak of their abilities. Unlike Beginning Learners, they are disinclined to engage in Low Effort – although there are times when they need to do this.

This type of learner spends their effort reproducing previous levels of performance. They avoid the risk of making errors above the line. They can be pushed above the line, but their distribution of effort is predominantly in the bottom right of the Effective Effort Matrix (see Figure 18: Effort – Performance Learners.).

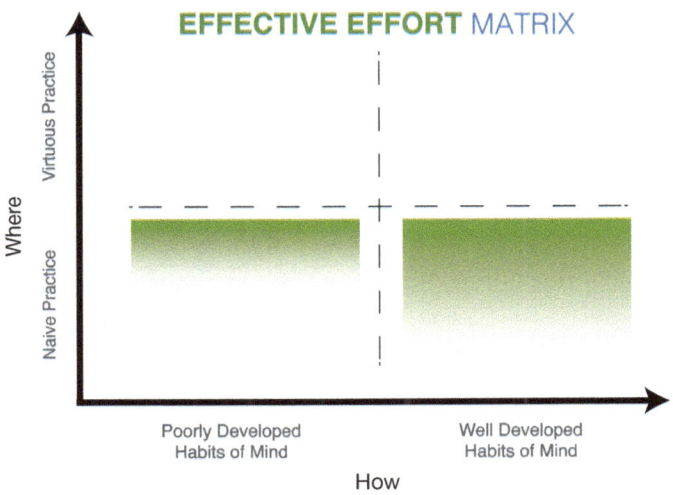

Figure 18: Effort – Performance Learners.

DIRECTED LEARNERS

Directed Learners spend their effort **producing** things – getting things completed. If directed to go above the line, they will do so. But much of their time is spent on Ineffective Effort. They are slow to identify Unproductive Struggle, and when they do, they tend to be slow to move into Productive Effort.

Given the opportunity, these learners will happily move below the bar, performing and cruising (see Figure 19: Effort – Directed Learners.).

THE LEARNING LANDSCAPE

These learners will, under direction, distribute their time towards the top left of the Effective Effort Matrix, with significant amounts of time also spent below the line.

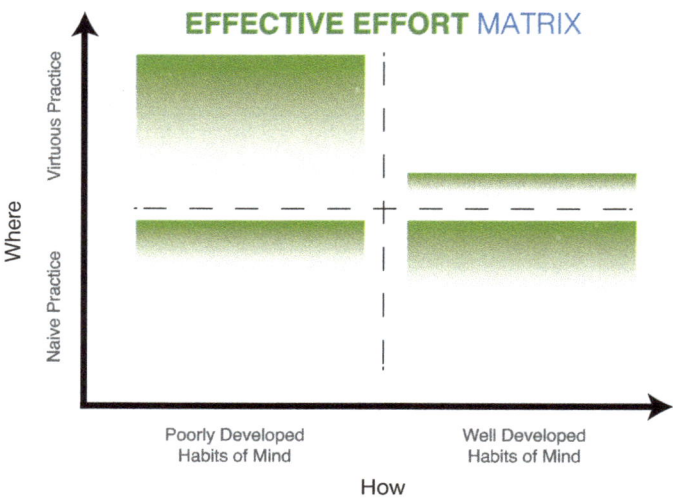

Figure 19: Effort – Directed Learners.

INDEPENDENT LEARNERS

Independent Learners spend their effort striving. As they are goal directed, they are less inclined to spend time below the line. They are better at discerning when they need to be in Performance Effort and seek to minimise the time they spend in Low Effort.

These learners are better at identifying Unproductive Struggle and are quicker to seek support and learn from mistakes, so they more readily shift to Effective Effort than Directed Learners.

These learners are focused above the line, so are less likely to spend time in Low Effort – although it is necessary to spend some time here. They spend the bulk of their time in the top left of the Effective Effort Matrix (see Figure 20: Effort – Independent Learners.).

CHAPTER 7: EFFORT

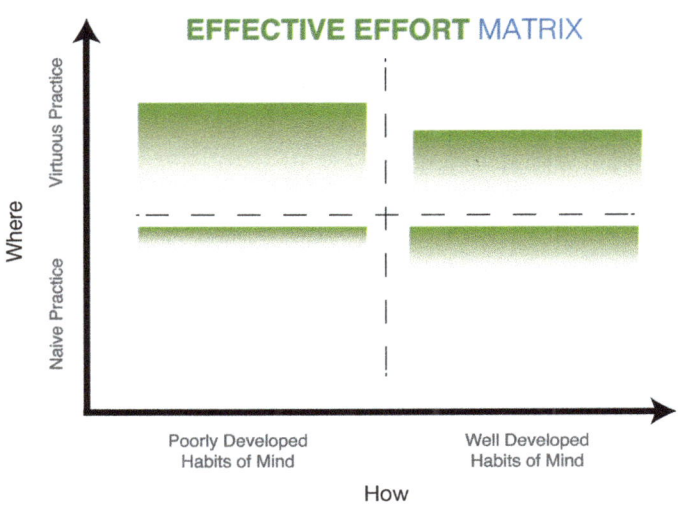

Figure 20: Effort – Independent Learners.

AGILE LEARNERS

Agile Learners spend most of their effort growing.

These learners are most clearly focused on increasing Learner Agency and becoming more effective learners. They know this doesn't happen below the line, so they seek to eliminate energy spent cruising. They are adept at identifying the situations that demand Performance Effort and expend energy in this quadrant only as required.

Agile Learners do not only focus their effort above the line – they are the most adept at shifting from Unproductive Struggle to Productive Struggle.

Agile Learners spend the maximum amount of effort in Effective Effort and, as a result, they are the most efficacious of all learners (see Figure 21: Effort – Agile Learners.).

THE LEARNING LANDSCAPE

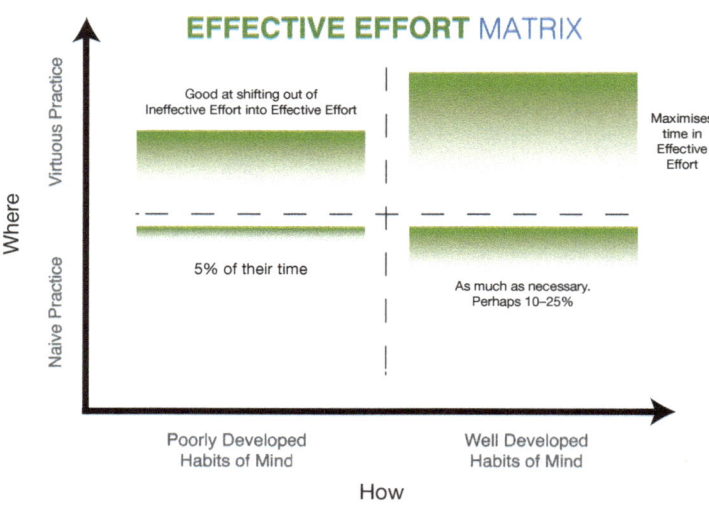

Figure 21: Effort – Agile Learners.

TEACHER ACTION: EFFORT

Help learners understand the different types of effort. Differentiate between spending time and energy on a task and the efficacy of that action. Ask students to develop posters and slogans that can be attached to the four different types of effort, so they can be recognised and discussed in the classroom.

Consider changing assessment practices that describe effort as high/low, satisfactory/unsatisfactory, etc., and shift to describing how different types of learners distribute their effort.

Avoid "praising effort" indiscriminately, confusing it with time and energy. Praise effort only when it's Effective Effort.

Focus praise on specific learner actions, such as taking on Learning Challenges, filling their backpacks by developing their Habits of Mind, responding to feedback, moving from Unproductive to Productive Struggle, recognising helpful and unhelpful mistakes, etc.

CHAPTER 7: EFFORT

Regularly ask students what types of effort they have been engaged in during a lesson, a day or a week. What percentage of their time do they spend in each type?

Consider using the different learner types to help students identify how they are using their time and energy and what they might do to improve.

CONCLUSION

The Learning Landscape is a metaphor for learning – but it is also more than that.

As we move through the Learning Landscape, we learn. Roaming far and wide, we discover new areas of knowledge, many of which we are familiar with in schools. As students, we explore the parts of the Learning Landscape we call languages, the arts, sciences, technology and maths. But the Learning Landscape doesn't stop with what we learn in school – it includes parenting, friendships, relationships and much more. The Learning Landscape includes all areas of knowledge and understanding.

Climbing higher in the Learning Landscape, we encounter more and more complex knowledge, building expertise as we climb. Those who stand atop the highest peaks are those we consider the best in their field.

Moving through the Learning Landscape and climbing higher is not a simple matter of putting one foot in front of the other. Learning involves succeeding at increasingly difficult challenges. Learning is a complex and difficult skill that all learners must develop to meet the increasing demands of these challenges.

Within the Learning Landscape, we recognise the best learners as the most skilful climbers. These learners are the best equipped. They have the biggest backpacks and the deepest understanding of the learning process. They no longer see the boundaries and limitations that less skilful learners see. They are able to move freely through the Learning Landscape and climb the peaks.

But there is one mountain in the Learning Landscape that we, as teachers, need to pay particular attention to. This is the mountain that represents our area of expertise – not our subject area expertise, but rather our understanding of the learning process itself. Above all else, teachers must be experts in the process of learning.

Throughout this book, we have described six different types of learners. These learners vary in their capacity to move through the Learning Landscape, as well as their attitudes towards critical aspects of learning, such as the Learning Zone, Habits

THE LEARNING LANDSCAPE

of Mind, Practice, Effort and a learner's mindset. As educators, we understand how different types of learners behave. More importantly, we must teach and guide these students to become better learners – it is not enough to merely identify how different learners behave.

Our school timetables often reflect the Learning Landscape, defining which part students will explore at a particular time. A skilful teacher uses this time not only to explore and teach students about an area of the Learning Landscape (which they may be an expert in), but they also use it to develop students as learners.

The Learning Landscape gives teachers a way of talking to learners about the process of learning. It is not an activity or a pedagogy. Rather, it is a metaphor that gives students and teachers a concrete, practical and powerful way of thinking about and discussing learning. The skilful teacher uses this metaphor not as a story, but as a tool.

As experts in learning, we identify a student's Learning Zone, for learning. That is, we identify their next step in becoming a better learner, then guide them on that journey. We show them how to become better learners!

For example, when we encounter a learner who we might identify as a Non-Learner, we acknowledge that they are ignorant of their learning behaviours. This "ignorance" doesn't define the individual. Rather, it defines how sophisticated they are as a learner. They have no vocabulary for their Habits of Mind. As educators, our role is to recognise that this learner's Learning Zone, for learning, is to build that vocabulary. So, we use the metaphor of the Learning Landscape to introduce the student to their backpack and give names to the tools we fill it with.

Once the student has built that vocabulary, their next step up the mountain of expertise we call "learning" is to understand when they are using those Habits of Mind. So, we teach them how to do this. As our lessons result in the student developing this ability, they climb higher up the mountain of learning, and we recognise them as a Beginning Learner.

Then, our job is to take them from Beginning Learner to Performance Learner. We guide the student in predicting and selecting the most appropriate Habits of Mind for what they are learning about.

Once the student has developed an understanding of the tools in their backpack, what they are and what they are used for, our next step is to help them develop an understanding of "how well" they are using the Habits of Mind. We guide the student to make the shift from "using" their Habits of Mind to understanding the need to

CONCLUSION

improve and get better at their Habits of Mind. As a Directed Learner, we start them on the journey of filling their backpack.

A similar journey of becoming a better learner could be described for how the learner responds to their Learning Zone, how they use mistakes and feedback as sources of information, and how they use their time and energy as effective effort.

The Learning Landscape gives us a language and a powerful visual metaphor for understanding learning and the learning process. Importantly, it helps us guide students to become better learners.

I invite you to use this metaphor in your classrooms. Encourage your students to explore the Learning Landscape, take on challenges and understand the effect different types of challenges have on their learning. Remove the imaginary boundaries created by the Fixed Mindset. Equip your students to climb the highest peaks. Help them recognise the important role mistakes and feedback have in the learning process. And ensure they understand that "effort" is more than time and energy spent on a task.

But most importantly, use this metaphor to help your learners climb the mountain of expertise that is learning. Use the Learning Landscape to guide them as you exercise your expertise – the process of ensuring your students become better learners!

GLOSSARY

ABOVE-THE-LINE LEARNER: An Above-the-Line Learner is someone who constantly stretches themselves to reach greater heights in the Learning Landscape. They attempt challenges that are in their Learning Zone and seek to increase their Learner Agency to succeed at these challenges.

ANTIFRAGILE: A term coined by Nassim Nicholas Taleb to describe something that benefits from disruption. Fragile things break when they encounter disruption, while robust or resilient things withstand or recover from disruption. Things that are antifragile benefit and grow as a result of disruption.

ASPIRATIONAL CHALLENGE: When the Far Side of the Challenge Pit is significantly higher than the Near Side, a learner faces an Aspirational Challenge. This type of challenge requires an increase in Learner Agency that is not possible to achieve in one go. As a result, it is impossible to succeed at Aspirational Challenges unless they are broken down into a series of smaller Learning Challenges. In this case, the Far Side of this pit is in the learner's Aspirational Zone.

ASPIRATIONAL ZONE: This zone lies beyond the Learning Zone. The Aspirational Zone represents challenges that are currently too difficult for the learner to attempt. They are too much of a stretch for the learner to succeed at in one step.

BACKPACK: A learner's backpack is where they store their Habits of Mind. The larger the backpack, the better equipped a learner is to confront increasingly difficult challenges in the Learning Landscape.

BACKSTORY: A backstory is another way of representing a learning journey. It represents the history of a learner's challenges through the Learning Landscape. The most successful learners have backstories that trace their journey up mountains of expertise.

THE LEARNING LANDSCAPE

BELOW-THE-LINE LEARNER: A Below-the-Line Learner consistently selects challenges that are in their Performance Zone or Comfort Zone. They fail to stretch themselves, and instead of building Learner Agency, they rely on their current abilities. These learners could be said to be only learning "more easy things they haven't done yet", never becoming better learners.

CHALLENGE: A challenge is represented by a Challenge Pit. The amount of challenge is determined by the difference between the Near Side and the Far Side of the Challenge Pit.

COMFORT ZONE: This zone refers to challenges that are well within the learner's current abilities. Challenges in this zone have either been mastered long ago or are "easy things the learner hasn't done yet".

CONTOUR LINES: In the Learning Landscape, contour lines represent height as well as the difficulty and complexity of the knowledge and understanding. The higher a contour line, the more difficult and complex the knowledge and understandings are.

DELIBERATE PRACTICE: A term used by Anders Ericsson to describe practice that focuses on growth and doing better than your current best (Learning Zone). Further, it is usually guided by an expert and occurs only in fields where there is a well-defined and agreed-upon standard of excellence. In the context of the Learning Landscape, it is when a learner is accompanied by an expert up the mountain of expertise, along a path that has been travelled by previous experts.

DOWNHILL CHALLENGE: When the Near Side of the Challenge Pit is higher than the Far Side, a learner faces a Downhill Challenge. This type of challenge results in the learner acquiring less complex and difficult knowledge and understandings, and requires no additional Learner Agency from the learner. The learner leaves the pit through their Comfort Zone.

EFFECTIVE EFFORT: Effective Effort leads to growth. It includes the development of more mature Habits of Mind, as well as the application of these Habits of Mind to succeed at challenges that are more difficult and complex than the learner has previously encountered.

EFFICACY PROBLEM: An Efficacy Problem occurs when a learner seeks to improve but engages in the wrong sorts of actions, incorrectly believing they will bring about growth. An Efficacy Problem is corrected by teaching students more efficacious actions.

GLOSSARY

FIXED MINDSET: The belief that your most basic characteristics, such as your talents, abilities and intelligence, are unchangeable and therefore represent a permanent limit to your abilities.

GROWTH MINDSET: The understanding that your most basic characteristics, such as your talents, abilities and intelligence, can be developed.

HABITS OF MIND: Described by Art Costa and Bena Kallick, the Habits of Mind are the dispositions that are skilfully and mindfully employed by characteristically successful learners when in their Learning Zone. In the context of the Learning Landscape, they are what goes in the learner's backpack to help them get out of a Challenge Pit.

IGNORANCE PROBLEM: An Ignorance Problem occurs when a learner either lacks or is given incorrect information about the nature of their abilities. For example, the learner may be unaware of their brain's ability to change and, therefore, create new abilities. Alternatively, the learner may be told that some individuals have special abilities that are unavailable to others. In both cases, the learner suffers from an Ignorance Problem that can be addressed by giving them accurate information.

INEFFECTIVE EFFORT: This type of effort occurs when a learner stretches themselves beyond their current best and attempts challenges in their Learning Zone, but fails to develop their Habits of Mind to the level required to succeed at these increasingly difficult tasks. As a result, they struggle. The struggle may be Unproductive Struggle resulting in stagnation, or Productive Struggle resulting in the slow development of their Habits of Mind and movement into Effective Effort.

LEARNER AGENCY: This is a measure of a learner's "power to act", a reflection of their ability to move through the Learning Landscape. The greater the Learner Agency, the more able the learner is to take on increasingly difficult challenges.

LEARNING CHALLENGE: When the Far Side of the Challenge Pit is slightly higher than the Near Side, a learner faces a Learning Challenge. This type of challenge results in the learner acquiring more complex and difficult knowledge and demands greater Learner Agency from the learner. The learner leaves the pit through their Learning Zone.

LEARNING JOURNEY: A learning journey represents the path a learner takes through the Learning Landscape. Each learner is likely to take a different path, and thus acquire different knowledge and understandings.

THE LEARNING LANDSCAPE

LEARNING LANDSCAPE: The Learning Landscape is a metaphor for where learning takes place. Everything that can be learned has a place in the Learning Landscape. As a learner travels through the Learning Landscape, they acquire new knowledge and understandings.

LEARNING PLATEAU: A Learning Plateau represents a level of difficulty (see Contour Lines) a learner has been stuck at for a period of time and may appear as a permanent limit. The Learning Plateau is set at the learner's current level of Learner Agency and cannot be exceeded without increasing their Learner Agency.

LEARNING ZONE: Sometimes referred to as "The Zone of Proximal Development", the Learning Zone represents a challenge that stretches a learner just beyond their current best. To succeed at a challenge in the Learning Zone, learners must first develop greater Learner Agency.

LOW EFFORT: We see Low Effort when a learner is engaged in challenges well below the line in their Comfort and Performance Zones. These types of challenges draw on only the most basic of the learner's Habits of Mind.

MINDSET CONTINUUM: Designed by the author, James Anderson, the Mindset Continuum fills the gap in our understanding of the Fixed and Growth Mindsets. It describes the graduated behaviours we observe in learners as they become increasingly growth oriented.

MINDSET MOVER: An experience that influences a learner's mindset, teaching them something about the nature of their most basic characteristics, such as their talents, abilities or intelligence. Mindset Movers can be positive, creating a more growth-oriented mindset, or they can be negative, creating a more fixed-oriented mindset.

MOTIVATION CALIBRATION: A learner with good motivation calibration not only understands that they are capable of growth but are also able to describe what actions will be required to achieve that growth. They are able to accurately "count the cost" of the growth.

PERCEPTION PROBLEM: A Perception Problem occurs when a learner fails to recognise their own growth, despite having achieved that growth. A Perception Problem may occur when educators use the same words (e.g. "A" or "at standard") to describe different standards. Because the same term is used, the learner may fail to see that they have grown.

GLOSSARY

PERFORMANCE CHALLENGE: When the Near Side and Far Side of the Challenge Pit are the same height, the learner faces a Performance Challenge. This type of challenge results in learning that is of the same difficulty and complexity the learner had previously acquired. The learner leaves the pit through their Performance Zone.

PERFORMANCE EFFORT: We see Performance Effort when a learner is engaged in doing "their best". They draw on their most well-developed Habits of Mind from their backpack and apply these to tasks in the Performance Zone.

PERFORMANCE ZONE: This zone represents a learner's current best. Challenges in this zone demand a learner call upon all their existing skills and abilities to perform at their highest possible standard.

PIT: A pit is a way of representing a challenge. Like getting into a pit, confronting a Challenge Pit can feel daunting. The level of challenge will depend on the shape of the pit (see Downhill, Learning, Performance and Aspirational Challenges).

PRODUCTIVE STRUGGLE: The hallmark of Productive Struggle is that it produces information that is discernible by the learner and helps them move from Ineffective Effort to Effective Effort.

PURPOSEFUL PRACTICE: Similar to Deliberate Practice, Purposeful Practice is focused on growth and doing better than the learner's best. But in this case, there may be no agreed-upon standards of excellence or others to guide the way. In the context of the Learning Landscape, it is about the learner finding their own path up a largely unexplored mountain of expertise.

THE LINE: Sometimes referred to as "the bar", the line represents a learner's current highest level of achievement. In the Learning Landscape, the line is represented by the highest point, or contour line, the learner has reached.

UNPRODUCTIVE STRUGGLE: The hallmark of Unproductive Struggle is that the amount of time and energy a learner spends on a challenge increases but progress stops. In this case, the learner is unable to discern any useful information from their efforts and fails to progress. When stuck in Unproductive Struggle, the learner either needs to seek additional sources of information (e.g. a teacher) or change the challenge, so it produces more useful information that will help them progress.

THE LEARNING LANDSCAPE

VIRTUOUS PRACTICE: A term that includes Deliberate Practice and Purposeful Practice. They share the common elements of being focused on growth and doing better than the learner's previous best. They both apply Ericsson's 3 Fs. Focus on what you are trying to achieve. Feedback on your progress and what mistakes are telling you. Fix It, correct your mistakes and master the new learning.

LIST OF FIGURES

FIGURE 1:	The Learning Plateau.	21
FIGURE 2:	Comfort Zone. Performance Zone. Learning Zone.	25
FIGURE 3:	The Challenge Pit – Near Side and Far Side	42
FIGURE 4:	The Challenge Pit – Zones.	44
FIGURE 5:	Downhill Challenge.	45
FIGURE 6:	Performance Challenge.	46
FIGURE 7:	Learning Challenge.	47
FIGURE 8:	Aspirational Challenge.	48
FIGURE 9:	Different Types of Challenges.	49
FIGURE 10:	Habits of Mind – Costa and Kallick's 16 Habits of Mind.	63
FIGURE 11:	The Mindset Continuum.	98
FIGURE 12:	Emotional Cascade of the Fixed Mindset.	100
FIGURE 13:	Emotional Cascade of the Growth Mindset.	101
FIGURE 14:	Beliefs, Actions and Experiences	103
FIGURE 15:	Effective Effort Matrix.	119
FIGURE 16:	Effort – Non-Learners.	122
FIGURE 17:	Effort – Beginning Learners.	122
FIGURE 18:	Effort – Performance Learners.	123
FIGURE 19:	Effort – Directed Learners.	124
FIGURE 20:	Effort – Independent Learners.	125
FIGURE 21:	Effort – Agile Learners.	126

ENDNOTES

1. Ericsson, K. A. (1996). *The Road to Excellence: The Acquisition of Expert Performance in the Arts and Sciences, Sports, and Games.* Mahwah, NJ: Lawrence Erlbaum Associates.
2. Ericsson, K. A. & Pool, R. (2016). *Peak: Secrets from the New Science of Expertise.* New York, NY: Houghton Mifflin Harcourt.
3. Ibid.
4. Ericsson, K. A. (1996). *The Road to Excellence: The Acquisition of Expert Performance in the Arts and Sciences, Sports, and Games.* Mahwah, NJ: Lawrence Erlbaum Associates.
5. Anderson, J. (2017). *The Agile Learner: Where Growth Mindset, Habits of Mind and Practice Unite.* Melbourne, Victoria: Hawker Brownlow Education.
6. Ericsson, K. A., Charness, N., Feltovich, P. J. & Hoffman, R. R. (2006). *The Cambridge Handbook of Expertise and Expert Performance.* NY, New York: Cambridge University Press.
7. Howe, M. J. A. (1999). *Genius Explained.* New York, NY: Cambridge University Press.
8. Ibid.
9. Ericsson, K. A. (1996). *The Road to Excellence: The Acquisition of Expert Performance in the Arts and Sciences, Sports, and Games.* Mahwah, NJ: Lawrence Erlbaum Associates.
10. Appleyard, B. (2009). Books That Helped to Change the World. *The Times,* [online]. Available at: https://www.thetimes.co.uk/article/books-that-helped-to-change-the-world-qbhxgvg2kwh [Accessed 3 Jul. 2019]
11. Taleb, N. N. (2012). *Antifragile: Things That Gain from Disorder.* New York, NY: Random House.
12. Vygotsky, L. S. (1978). *Mind in Society: The Development of Higher Psychological Processes.* Cambridge, MA: Harvard University Press.
13. Tan, B. H. & Galea, S. R. (eds.) (2009). *Proceedings of the 14th International Conference on Thinking and Learning 2009.* Kuala Lumpur: Universiti Putra Malaysia.
14. Edwards, J. & Martin, B. (2004). *Transformational Learning.* [image]. Available at: http://slideplayer.com/slide/8707365/26/images/13/TRANSFORMATIONAL+LEARNING.jpg [Accessed 4 Jul. 2019]
15. Nottingham, J. (2010). *Challenging Learning: Theory, Effective Practice and Lesson Ideas to Create Optimal Learning in the Classroom.* Cramlington, UK: JN Publishing Ltd.
16. Ericsson, K. A. & Pool, R. (2016). *Peak: Secrets from the New Science of Expertise.* New York, NY: Houghton Mifflin Harcourt.
17. Vygotsky, L. S. (1978). *Mind in Society: The Development of Higher Psychological Processes.* Cambridge, MA: Harvard University Press.
18. Tan, B. H. & Galea, S. R. (eds.) (2009). *Proceedings of the 14th International Conference on Thinking and Learning 2009.* Kuala Lumpur: Universiti Putra Malaysia.
19. Edwards, J. & Martin, B. (2004). *Transformational Learning.* [image]. Available at: http://slideplayer.com/slide/8707365/26/images/13/TRANSFORMATIONAL+LEARNING.jpg [Accessed 4 Jul. 2019]
20. Nottingham, J. (2010). *Challenging Learning: Theory, Effective Practice and Lesson Ideas to Create Optimal Learning in the Classroom.* Cramlington, UK: JN Publishing Ltd.
21. Ericsson, K. A. & Pool, R. (2016). *Peak: Secrets from the New Science of Expertise.* New York, NY: Houghton Mifflin Harcourt.
22. Costa, A. L. & Kallick, B. (2008). *Learning and Leading with Habits of Mind: 16 Essential Characteristics for Success.* Alexandria, VA: ASCD.
23. Anderson, J. (2010). *Succeeding with Habits of Mind: Developing, Infusing and Sustaining the Habits of Mind for a More Thoughtful Classroom.* Melbourne, Victoria: Hawker Brownlow Education.
24. De Bono, E. (2016). *Lateral Thinking.* London, UK: Penguin Books.
25. turiaschampions.com, (2018). Turia's Champions. [online] Available at: https://www.turiaschampions.com/ [Accessed 3 Jul. 2019]
26. Ericsson, K. A. & Pool, R. (2016). *Peak: Secrets from the New Science of Expertise.* New York, NY: Houghton Mifflin Harcourt.
27. Ibid.
28. Anderson, J. (2017). *The Agile Learner: Where Growth Mindset, Habits of Mind and Practice Unite.* Melbourne, Victoria: Hawker Brownlow Education.
29. Ericsson, K. A. & Pool, R. (2016). *Peak: Secrets from the New Science of Expertise.* New York, NY: Houghton Mifflin Harcourt.
30. Ibid.

31. Ibid.
32. Briceño, E. (2018). Mistakes Are Not All Created Equal. [blog] *Mindset Works*. Available at: http://blog.mindsetworks.com/entry/mistakes-are-not-all-created-equal [Accessed 19 Aug. 2019]
33. Anderson, J. (2017). The Agile Learner: Where Growth Mindset, Habits of Mind and Practice Unite. Melbourne, Victoria: Hawker Brownlow Education.
34. *Roger Federer: Never Stop Improving*. (2017). [video] Montréal, Quebec: Goalcast.
35. Ericsson, K. A. & Pool, R. (2016). *Peak: Secrets from the New Science of Expertise*. New York, NY: Houghton Mifflin Harcourt.
36. Dweck, C. (2006). *Mindset: The New Psychology of Success*. New York, NY: Random House.
37. Ericsson, K. A. & Pool, R. (2016). *Peak: Secrets from the New Science of Expertise*. New York, NY: Houghton Mifflin Harcourt.
38. *Roger Federer: Never Stop Improving*. (2017). [video] Montréal, Quebec: Goalcast
39. Anderson, J. (2017). *The Agile Learner: Where Growth Mindset, Habits of Mind and Practice Unite*. Melbourne, Victoria: Hawker Brownlow Education.
40. Sisk, V., Burgoyne, A., Sun, J., Butler, J. & Macnamara, B. (2018). To What Extent and Under Which Circumstances Are Growth Mind-Sets Important to Academic Achievement? Two Meta-Analyses. *Psychological Science* [online] Volume 29(4), pp. 549-571. Available at: https://journals.sagepub.com/doi/abs/10.1177/0956797617739704?journalCode=pssa [Accessed 4 Jun. 2019]
41. Mourshed, M., Krawitz, M. & Dorn, E. (2017). *How to Improve Student Educational Outcomes: New Insights from Data Analytics*. [online] New York, NY: McKinsey & Company. Available at: https://www.mckinsey.com/industries/social-sector/our-insights/how-to-improve-student-educational-outcomes-new-insights-from-data-analytics [Accessed 4 Jun. 2019]

ABOUT THE AUTHOR

James Anderson is an Australian-based international speaker, author and educator who is passionate about helping fellow educators develop students as better learners. Originally a teacher and school leader, for the past 20 years, James has been working with schools to make classrooms more thoughtful places.

In his school-based consultancy, workshops and online resources, James provides the "follow-through" that's so often lacking in teacher professional development. He provides not only the deep understandings required to do this work meaningfully, but also the practical tools and ongoing support needed to sustain change your school and make a real difference to student learning outcomes.

James regularly speaks at conferences around the world. His previous publications include *Succeeding with Habits of Mind*, *The Agile Learner* and *The Mindset Continuum*, as well as a host of ebooks and other teacher resources. His online course, "Transforming Teaching and Learning with Growth Mindsets," supports thousands of educators in schools around the world. He is an international affiliate of Art Costa and Bena Kallick's Institute for Habits of Mind and the creator of www.habitsofmind.org.

James can be contacted for speaking and consultancy work at jamesanderson.com.au.

THE AGILE LEARNER

Where **Growth Mindset**, **Habits of Mind** and **Practice** *Unite*

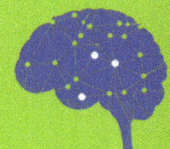

The Agile Learner unites three powerful ideas: Growth Mindset, Habits of Mind and Virtuous Practice.

A Growth Mindset is the understanding that we can change our most basic characteristics such as our talents and abilities. But achieving that *Growth* requires more than simply the right mindset, it requires the right actions.

In The *Agile Learner* you'll discover how to change your students' mindsets by moving them along the Mindset Continuum. Importantly, you'll learn how to engage students in the processes and behaviours that achieve growth and the development of new talents.

Succeeding with Habits of Mind

Beginning your learning journey with Habits of Mind is easy. Knowing where the next steps are can be elusive, and more challenging. In these pages you'll find practical guidance that takes you beyond introducing the Habits of Mind and helps you build deep understandings so you can succeed in developing, infusing, leading and sustaining the Habits of Mind in your school. You will learn how to: Develop students' Habits of Mind; Infuse the Habits of Mind into the curriculum; Lead the change in your school; Sustain the change; and Connect with others. Success is a journey. This book gives you the knowledge you'll need as you move beyond the basics and succeed in building an even more thoughtful learning community with Habits of Mind.